Questions & Answers
Criminal Law

CAROLINA ACADEMIC PRESS
Questions & Answers Series

Questions & Answers
Criminal Law

Multiple Choice and Short Answer
Questions and Answers

FIFTH EDITION

Paul Marcus

HAYNES PROFESSOR OF LAW EMERITUS

THE COLLEGE OF WILLIAM & MARY

CAROLINA ACADEMIC PRESS

Durham, North Carolina

LIBRARY OF CONGRESS CATALOGING-IN-PUBLICATION DATA

ISBN   978-1-5310-2296-9
eISBN   978-1-5310-2297-6
LCCN   2022947958

Carolina Academic Press
700 Kent Street
Durham, North Carolina 27701
(919) 489-7486
www.cap-press.com

Printed in the United States of America

Contents

About the Author

Paul Marcus is the Haynes Professor of Law Emeritus, at the College of William and Mary, Williamsburg, Virginia. He has written casebooks and treatises in both criminal law and criminal procedure, and has lectured on these topics throughout the United States and in many foreign nations as well. He is the former Law Dean at the University of Arizona, and Interim Law Dean at William and Mary.

Preface

The study of criminal law in the first year of law school (for most students) involves a rich overview of the United States criminal justice system, explores questions as to why, whom and how we punish, and requires us to face squarely the relationship of the individual to the state. The issues considered in the class are some of the most disturbing and important found throughout the law school curriculum: What are the limits on the ability of the state to sanction behavior? What is appropriate punishment for crimes? What evidence is sufficient to demonstrate a culpable state of mind? Why are victims of some awful offenses so reluctant to report the crimes? Should we have a felony murder rule? Does it make sense to establish degrees of murder? Is the crime of conspiracy which casts a wide net of criminal responsibility, justified? In relieving defendants of responsibility, have we as a society grown to rely too heavily on defenses such as self-defense, necessity, entrapment and insanity?

The key to learning criminal law is to ask, and then answer, several questions about each problem. These include:

1. What crime is charged — the answer is not always self-evident, as the differences between crimes such as second degree murder and involuntary manslaughter, for instance, can be subtle.

2. Is the crime within the permissible scope of legislative action — are there some activities which simply cannot be prohibited by the state?

3. What are the elements of the crime — laying out the elements of "actus reus", "mens rea" and causation usually is not difficult, defining particular elements (such as the act requirement for the attempt offense) can be very tough.

4. What is the standard of review to determine if the case can proceed — has the government offered sufficient evidence such that a reasonable person could find all the elements of the crime, beyond a reasonable doubt?

5. What evidence has the government brought forth to prove its case — often the prosecution will base its theory heavily, if not entirely, on circumstantial evidence while defense counsel will argue that such evidence is not persuasive.

6. Can the defendant rebut the government's case by offering evidence of an affirmative defense — some of the defenses play a large role in the determination of criminal responsibility.

In answering these questions, I encourage you to do so as carefully as you can, whether in responding with short answers or in analyzing the multiple choices given. Your inclination might be to look at the question, think briefly about the answer, and then read the one that I have prepared. Going through the question thoroughly, however, will prove far more beneficial to you in developing your understanding of the underlying issues presented in the questions.

While the questions and answers you will read in this book contain a considerable amount of information, the purpose here is not to teach a short course in criminal law. Rather, I hope these materials will test your knowledge of the key principles in the subject and how they ought to be viewed as a whole. The book is designed as a supplement to the course casebook you will be assigned by your criminal law professor. You will find questions and answers in seven principal subject areas that correspond to the main topics many teachers cover in the introductory criminal law course: Limits on the Criminal Sanction, Elements of the Offense, Parties to Crimes, Inchoate Offenses, Crimes, Causation, and Defenses. This book is organized in much the same way as many of the more popular criminal law casebooks. Still, even if your professor covers the material in a different order the book should be helpful to you.

The problems in this book are not keyed to any one body of criminal law such as Federal law, the Model Penal Code or any one or more particular states. Instead, the problems are based on majority principles, with notations as to significant minority views or developing modern trends.

I wish you good luck with your study of the fascinating and important matters you will see in your criminal law course.

Paul Marcus
Williamsburg, VA
June 2022

Questions

Limits on the Criminal Sanction

1. Responding to merchant complaints about addicts congregating by fancy stores, the legislature passed a new law making it a crime "to be addicted to the use of illegal narcotics." Walking on the public street, Dawn was seen by a police officer moving unsteadily. The officer approached Dawn and asked her, "Are you O.K.?" Dawn replied, "None of your business." The officer observed fresh needle marks on Dawn's arm while she said, "I really need my stuff, don't arrest me." Dawn was arrested and charged with violating the new law.

   Can she be successfully prosecuted?

   A. Yes, the officer's observations are sufficient evidence to convict Dawn.

   B. Yes, the officer's observations, coupled with Dawn's statements, are ample evidence to convict.

   C. No, a conviction would violate Dawn's constitutional rights.

   D. No, Dawn's statement cannot be used against her.

2. Could Dawn be successfully prosecuted for the crime of being under the influence of narcotics while in public?

   ANSWER:

3. Does the result above change if Dawn offered convincing evidence both that she was addicted to narcotics and that she was a homeless person who was on the street because she had no other alternative?

   A. Yes. Because Dawn is an addict and homeless, punishing her for this crime when she has nowhere else to go would violate the Constitution.

   B. Yes. Because Dawn is an addict and her disease compels her to take drugs, it would be cruel and unusual punishment to convict her for her status, rather than for a voluntary action that she undertook.

   C. Yes, if Dawn was not aware that being under the influence in public was illegal, even if this law was published in the state code.

D. No. Although Dawn is an addict, she does not lack free will. Because she could choose not to take drugs or not to do so in a public place, convicting her of being under the influence in public would not be prohibited.

4. Alexander was evicted from his apartment in Los Angeles. As a result, he has been temporarily seeking shelter in an empty storefront's entryway on the sidewalk while he waits to find housing or for shelter to become available. The City of Los Angeles has received complaints about people sitting and laying on the city sidewalks. Can the city respond to these complaints by passing a law that would arrest people who are found sleeping and sitting on Los Angeles city sidewalks?

ANSWER:

5. Suppose Alexander has relocated from the storefront to a local park. There is a city ordinance preventing overnight camping inside the park. Police officers approach Alexander to enforce the ordinance. Once they discover Alexander is houseless, the officers inform him that there is a nearby shelter with availability. Alexander does not want to go to the shelter. What can the officers do?

   A. The officers can force Alexander to go to the shelter, citing concerns for his safety.

   B. The officers can arrest Alexander for violating the ordinance.

   C. The officers cannot arrest Alexander for violating the ordinance because he is houseless.

   D. The officers can arrest Alexander for being voluntarily houseless.

6. Bashira was speeding down the road. An officer arrested her for "unsafe driving," based on the observation of her speeding and her erratic lane changing. Bashira's lawyer asserts that the statute should be declared void for vagueness, insofar as the state legislature never defined what actions were intended to be prohibited in the law. Should the judge find the statute unconstitutional?

ANSWER:

7. Would the result change if the statute referred to "reckless driving" instead of "unsafe driving"?

ANSWER:

Elements of the Offense

THE ACT

Failure to Act

8. Zion was driving home after a long day of work. As he was exiting the highway, he saw a car that had not slowed down enough for the off ramp. The car had run into the highway sound wall and the accident looked fairly serious. Certain that someone had already reported the accident, and anxious to get home, Zion did not stop and offer assistance. Unfortunately, no one reported the accident until several hours after Zion passed by and the driver died from internal bleeding before reaching the hospital. If the police learn that Zion drove by the accident, but did not intervene or call 911, can he be held criminally liable?

   A. Yes. Given the seriousness of the accident, the victim was clearly in grave danger and Zion owed a duty to help the driver.

   B. Yes. Because Zion may have been the last person able to call or intervene in time to prevent the driver from dying, he can be held liable for failing to do so.

   C. No. Only medical professionals can be required to help the driver.

   D. No. There is no general duty for a person to assist others.

9. Would the result change if Zion were a highway patrol officer who passed the accident and chose not to stop or phone in a report because his shift was about to end and he wanted to get home?

   ANSWER:

10. Troy was involved in a car accident in which the driver of the other car was seriously injured. Fearful that he would be unfairly blamed for the collision, Troy drove away without rendering aid or reporting the accident. Can Troy be successfully prosecuted for his conduct *after* the accident?

    A. Yes, being in the accident created a greater moral obligation on Troy's part.

    B. Yes, most states require immediate assistance and or reporting after being in an accident.

    C. No, there is no general duty to assist others.

    D. No, Troy was under no duty to assist others because he was not at fault in causing the collision.

11. Matthew and his ex-wife had been divorced for two years. They had joint custody of their young children and the children often spent weekends away with their mother. On several occasions, after they returned to his home, Matthew noticed burn marks on his daughter's arm. When he asked his daughter about this, she said that sometimes she was a bad girl and her mother had to punish her. Matthew knew that his wife had been violent with the children in the past. However, he was scared of starting another custody battle with his ex-wife because she had threatened to "dig up some dirt" on him. Matthew did not bring up the issue with his ex or with anyone else. Can Matthew be held criminally liable for the harm to the child?

    A. Yes, because of his special relationship with his children, Matthew's failure to act makes him responsible for their abuse.

    B. Yes, because he chose to become involved when he asked his daughter about her injuries.

    C. No, because Matthew had no affirmative duty to act, and he had no direct role in inflicting the abuse.

    D. No. Matthew's ex-wife is the truly culpable party in this situation.

12. Would the result in the above problem change if Matthew was not the girl's father, but instead was her teacher?

13. Marianna harbored a deep hatred of her sister Katherine. After years of growing resentment, Marianna was consumed with jealousy of her more successful, intelligent, and attractive sister. She began to craft an elaborate plan to kill her sister. However, before she took any steps to commit the murder, her plot was discovered. Can Marianna be held criminally liable for her scheme?

ANSWER:

The Voluntary Act

14. Betty drove two of her friends home from work. On the drive, she lost control of the car and slammed into a big tree. The two friends were both killed. Apparently, while driving, Betty lost consciousness and ran off the road. A later medical examination indicates that Betty had an undiagnosed brain disorder in the portion of her brain that regulates consciousness, and this disorder very likely caused her to become unconscious while driving. Can Betty be held criminally responsible for the deaths of her friends?

   A. No, because the law only punishes people for voluntary acts and Betty did not act voluntarily when she slammed into the tree.

   B. No, because Betty was only offering assistance in driving the others and the law does not punish good Samaritans.

   C. Yes, because Betty could still be convicted even without a voluntary act.

   D. Yes, because Betty committed a voluntary act when she agreed to drive passengers.

15. Would the result in the above problem change if Betty knew of her medical problem but decided to drive anyway because it was such a short ride?

16. Would the result in problem 14 change if, at trial, the judge instructed the jury that in order to avoid conviction Betty needed to show—by a preponderance of the evidence—that she was not conscious at the time the car was involved in the accident?

   ANSWER:

17. Two police officers arrived at a downtown apartment house in response to complaints from neighbors about a noisy party. Binh answered the door, clearly inebriated. The officers told him to step outside to the sidewalk so that they could talk to him, insinuating that he would get into trouble if he did not do as told. When Binh went outside to speak with the officers and he reached the sidewalk, the officers arrested him for being drunk in public. Can Binh be convicted?

   A. Yes, because the statute does not require a voluntary act.

   B. Yes, because Binh committed the voluntary act when he drank alcohol.

   C. No, because a voluntary act requirement will be implied, and Binh did not act in such a manner as to violate the statute.

   D. No, because even if a voluntary act requirement is implied, Binh did not violate the statute.

18. Elise is a supervisor at construction sites. She recently underwent a surgical procedure and has been prescribed medication for her recovery. The bottle of pills warned against drinking or operating heavy machinery while taking the medication. There was a work emergency, and Elise felt pressured to come back to work, even though her doctor advised her to stay home and heal and to follow the instructions on her medication's label. While operating a crane, Elise got lightheaded from her medication and accidentally and involuntarily released the crane, causing injury to her coworkers on site. Can she be held criminally liable for this unfortunate accident?

ANSWER:

19. Would the result above change if, instead of experiencing lightheadedness from medication, Elise just fell asleep due to responding to a midnight work emergency when she was tired? Suppose the rest of the facts are the same. Elise fell asleep, causing her to involuntarily release the crane and injure her coworkers. If there was no underlying surgery or medical condition, can Elise still be held criminally responsible for falling asleep due to tiredness while on the job?

THE MENTAL STATE

20. For two years, Rick had been leaving his two young daughters in the care of his live-in girlfriend, Tamika. Though Tamika had a nasty temper, Rick loved her. The situation worked out well for him because he worked nights and the girls could remain at home with Tamika. One morning when he returned home from work, his oldest daughter was on the living room floor, crying, in obvious pain. Tamika claimed nothing odd had occurred the previous night. After the girl's condition did not improve throughout the day, Rick grew concerned that she was very sick and brought her to the hospital. The emergency room doctor determined that the girl had been beaten in the abdomen and severely injured. Tamika fled and was never found. Rick was later charged with felony child abuse, for "knowingly subjecting a child to significant injury or neglect." If the state demonstrates that Rick's younger child had been treated for a similar injury while staying with Tamika several months before this incident, could Rick be convicted on this charge?

A. No, because Rick had no way to know his girlfriend might be abusing his daughter.

B. No, because it is unfair to hold Rick responsible for the actions of his girlfriend.

C. Yes, because the previous incident — combined with his awareness of Tamika's temper — means that Rick knew his girlfriend could be violent and posed a serious risk to his daughters.

D. No, because the evidence could not establish that Rick had knowledge of a serious risk.

21. Would the result in the above problem change if Rick's child had not been injured before?

ANSWER:

22. Ellie, a very petite woman, went to the unofficial office happy hour after work. Although she was not generally a drinker, she frequently attended the nightly happy hour to get to know other people in the firm. During the course of her 45-minute stay, Ellie had one glass of white wine. On her short drive home, a police officer lawfully pulled her over. Suspecting Ellie was drunk, the officer conducted a field sobriety test. Ellie's blood alcohol was just above the legal limit. Which of the following arguments might successfully be put forth in her defense to a charge of driving under the influence?

    A. She did not know she was intoxicated.

    B. She did not intend to drive while intoxicated.

    C. Any reasonable person would have acted in the same manner, considering the circumstances.

    D. None of the above.

23. Suppose a child darted out into the road in front of Ellie, who was driving very fast. Although Ellie applied the brakes, she still hit the child and caused serious injuries. Fortunately, the child did not die as a result of the accident. What crime, in addition to any crime relating to driving under the influence, might Ellie be found guilty of due to the accident?

    A. Attempted murder.

    B. Reckless endangerment.

    C. Manslaughter.

    D. Negligent homicide.

24. While drinking in a bar, Mauricio got angry at another patron's insults and tried to punch him. The man ducked, however, and Mauricio accidentally punched a woman standing behind him, breaking her nose. Mauricio is charged with battery, which requires an "intentional act to injure another through physical contact." Will he be found guilty?

    A. Yes, because even if Mauricio did not intend to hit the person injured, he did intend to hit another person.

B. Yes, because the intent to hit someone is unnecessary.

C. No, because Mauricio did not intend to hit the person injured.

D. No, because Mauricio's intent to hit the man who insulted him was justified.

25. Kayla often visited her ailing uncle in prison. She was having a drink one afternoon and told the barkeep at the local pub that on Sundays she visited the penitentiary. The bartender asked if, while she was visiting, she would visit *his* uncle and give him the weather report. Kayla thought this was a bit odd, but the bartender assured her that his uncle used to travel a lot and just liked to hear about the weather in cities he knew. The bartender promised to provide her the weather information every week if she would give his uncle the message. The weather reports Kayla later conveyed seemed to make the bartender's uncle very happy. Kayla was ultimately charged with "knowingly assisting organized crime." The government asserts that the weather reports were actually coded messages about the activities of a local crime syndicate. Kayla claimed she did not know anything about any criminal activity, and the prosecution does not challenge her claim. If she truly did not know about the secret nature of the messages, could she be convicted?

    A. Yes, because she knew that she was delivering information, which in fact assisted the syndicate.

    B. Yes, because the knowledge requirement includes an objective evaluation, and a reasonable person would have known that these messages were not innocuous.

    C. No, because Kayla did not in fact know that the weather reports were assisting the criminal activity.

    D. No, because Kayla should only be held liable if she intended to assist the syndicate.

26. Randy owned an alpaca farm. Because the alpacas were very valuable, Randy strung an electric wire along the top of his fence to prevent thefts. He placed a small sign next to the generator for the electric fence wire, warning about possible electric shocks. Randy did not put up any other signs because he lived in the country and did not have any close neighbors. Some girl scouts were out hiking on adjacent land and one of the girls ran over to see the unusual looking alpacas. The girl climbed up on the fence to get a better look and grabbed the wire to steady herself. The electric shock caused her to fall off of the fence. She hit her head on a rock when she landed, causing injury.

    Can Randy be found guilty under a statute criminalizing "reckless behavior on one's property which results in an injury to others"?

    A. Yes. Randy should have seen the inherent risk in installing an electric fence without putting up several warning signs.

    B. Yes. Randy's behavior created a substantial and unjustifiable risk.

C. No. Although his behavior created an unjustifiable risk, Randy did not know that girl scouts frequented the area and was thus unaware of the risk.

D. No. It is not clear that Randy's actions, as opposed to the inattentive troop leader's actions, led to the girl's injuries.

27. Victoria got into a heated argument with her boyfriend. Eventually, the boyfriend ran at her with a large chef's knife. Victoria wrestled it away from him, but during the struggle the knife fell and badly cut the boyfriend's foot, resulting in serious injury. Putting aside any affirmative defenses, can Victoria be convicted of intentional wounding?

ANSWER:

28. Would the result in the above problem change if, just before the knife fell, Victoria yelled, "Now you are going to get it"?

29. Trisha went out to a bar with some friends and got extremely drunk. She and her companions shared a cab ride home. When Trisha arrived at her apartment house, she was unable to get in her door because her key kept getting jammed in the lock. As she had done on several previous occasions, she pried open the screen on the outside window and climbed inside. Once she was in the living room, a police officer arrived. Apparently, Trisha had mistakenly broken into her neighbor's apartment. She was arrested for attempted burglary. Can Trisha successfully defend herself by claiming she was just mistaken and thought that she was breaking into her own apartment?

A. Yes, such a mistake of fact can act as a defense.

B. Yes, mistake of fact can be offered to disprove that she had intended a burglary.

C. No, Trisha was mistaken only as to the apartment she entered, not as to her actions.

D. No, because a mistake of law is not a defense.

30. Ivan was charged with attempted murder after he planted a bomb on a commuter train full of people. The bomb was inoperable, as it did not have a necessary component that would allow it to detonate. Although the bomb was harmless, there was much media coverage of its discovery because the train was filled with hundreds of people. Ivan asserts that he knew the bomb would not work and that he wanted merely to show that security measures are lacking in the country's transportation system. If he is believed, will this argument allow him to successfully rebut the government's case for attempted murder?

ANSWER:

31. Would the result in the problem above change if the defendant was charged with reckless endangerment after several people were hurt jumping from the train in response to a porter screaming, "Look out, there's a bomb on board"?

32. Jorge owned a manufacturing plant. He realized that it would be much cheaper to dump polluted water from the manufacturing process into the adjacent river rather than pipe the water through an expensive filtering process. He asked his lawyer Delia whether it would violate any laws at all to dump the water into the river. Delia assured him, in an opinion letter, that such action would not violate the law. After dumping the water into the river, Jorge was prosecuted for polluting river water. Will his reliance on Delia's advice defeat the charge?

    A. Yes, Jorge's reliance was reasonable.

    B. Yes, he did not realize it was against the law to dump the water into the river.

    C. No, relying on the advice of a lawyer generally cannot be used against a criminal charge.

    D. No, the crime is likely a strict liability offense.

33. Would the answer to the question above change if Jorge relied on the statement to him made by the head of the State Attorney General's Office on Environmental Control, instead of by his own lawyer?

ANSWER:

Parties to Crimes

34. Tabitha's boyfriend told her about his plan to rob a bank with a friend. Although Tabitha expressed concerns about the scheme, especially that they might get caught and go to prison, she did not do anything to stop her boyfriend from carrying out his plan. Several days before the robbery was to take place, Tabitha's boyfriend asked her if she would go to the coffee shop next to the bank, sit outside, and alert him if anything untoward happened outside while the robbery was taking place. Tabitha agreed and did so on the day of the robbery. The robbery was interrupted in the process and the actors were arrested and charged. Under common law rules, can Tabitha be held responsible as a party to the robbery?

    A. No, she cannot be held liable as a party to the crime because she was not directly involved in the criminal enterprise.

    B. Yes, she can be held liable as a principal in the first degree.

    C. Yes, she can be held liable as a principal in the second degree.

    D. Yes, she can be held responsible as an accessory before the fact.

35. Assume that in the above example, Tabitha's boyfriend never told her of his plan to rob the bank. Tabitha did not act as a lookout, nor did she know of her boyfriend's desire to commit such a crime. Her boyfriend and a couple of his buddies showed up at Tabitha's apartment after the robbery and asked her if they could all go to her parents' mountain cabin for a week or so. Tabitha was surprised and she asked, "What's the hurry?" Her boyfriend told her that he and his friends had just robbed a bank and they needed to get out of town and lay low for a while. Tabitha laughed at them, assuming that he was joking with her. Tabitha consented and the group went to the cabin for a week. Several months later, Tabitha's boyfriend and his friends were arrested for the robbery. Under the modern approach, can Tabitha be found to be a party to the robbery? Would the result change if Tabitha knew that her boyfriend robbed two banks in the past?

ANSWER:

36. Sophie came home to find her wife, Bao, very upset. When she asked her what was wrong, Bao told her that an auto shop employee had yelled at her when she had her car inspected earlier that afternoon. Sophie was furious and stopped by the auto shop the next day. She asked to speak with the manager and demanded to know the name of the employee on duty the previous afternoon. The manager told Sophie the employee's name, and Sophie reported the incident. The manager seemed unconcerned, and Sophie got the impression that the manager did not believe the story. Before Sophie left the shop she said, "If you won't do anything about this, then I will!" She looked up the employee's address and went to his house to confront him about the incident. After the employee denied ever yelling at Sophie's wife, Sophie punched the employee. The blow knocked him out and he had to be treated for a concussion at the local hospital. Can the manager of the auto shop be convicted as a party to the battery under the modern approach?

A. Yes. The manager supplied Sophie with the name of the employee. Without knowing the employee's name, Sophie could not have found out where he lived.

B. Yes. Not only did the manager supply Sophie with the employee's name, but he was well aware of Sophie's intentions because of the statement Sophie made before leaving the auto shop.

C. No. Merely supplying the name of the employee is not sufficient aid for accomplice liability.

D. No. The manager was unaware of Sophie's intent to assault the employee at the time the manager gave out the employee's name.

37. Does the result in the previous question change if the manager supplied Sophie the name *after* knowing Sophie's intentions?

ANSWER:

38. Aisha intended to help Jason commit a burglary. Low on cash, she agreed to drive him to the house of his choice in exchange for a cut of the proceeds. Aisha drove and Jason went into the house and returned to the car about 30 minutes later with some goods from the house. Later, Aisha discovered that, in addition to stealing a few items from the house, Jason also pistol whipped a woman who was inside. Can Aisha be held liable as an accomplice in the assault?

A. No, because Aisha did not intend for the assault to be committed.

B. No, because Aisha did not commit an act in furtherance of the assault.

C. Yes, because Aisha intended that a crime be committed.

D. Yes, Aisha is liable as a partner in crime even though she did not know all of her partner's intentions.

39. In the above problem, assume that Jason intended only to burglarize the house and that he did not assault the woman inside. Instead, while Jason was in the process of gathering valuables, the owner of the house surprised Jason and pointed a gun at him. Jason reacted by shooting the owner of the house. The owner died instantly. Will Aisha be liable for the murder of the house's owner?

ANSWER:

40. Amanda and Lance often had lunch together and discussed their workplace gripes. One afternoon, Lance described how his boss repeatedly berated and humiliated him. Lance said that he'd love to make his boss "pay" for the way she treated him. Amanda, sympathetic to her friend's story, agreed, remarking, "It's not like she doesn't deserve it. I heard she treats her family the same way. She has something coming to her." A few days later, Lance attempted to cut the brake line in his boss' car, hoping that the car would wreck and that his boss would get into a serious accident. Lance was arrested for tampering with his boss' car. Did the conversation in the lunchroom provide for criminal liability on Amanda's part?

    A. Yes, because Amanda intended to encourage Lance to take the action he did.

    B. Yes, because Amanda encouraged Lance to take such an action.

    C. No, because the First Amendment protects freedom of speech.

    D. No, because Amanda likely did not have the requisite intent for Lance to commit the crime.

41. Jenkins, Al, and Chen conceived a plan to make some quick cash. They decided to kidnap the young son of a player for the city's professional football team. In order to assure they would not run into the father, a big 320-pound offensive tackle, they carefully timed the kidnapping on an away game weekend. On the appointed day, Al did not show up, but Jenkins and Chen decided to go ahead with the plan without him. Although the house was in a gated community, Jenkins and Chen were able to get past the gate in Jenkins' work van under the pretense of fixing a resident's plumbing. They snatched the boy from the front driveway where he was playing and drove several hundred miles to a remote part of the state. The boy was obviously very upset, and Chen began to feel sorry for him. He told Jenkins that they should give up the scheme. He pointed out that Al knew all of their plans and location and might try to claim a reward and turn them in. Although Jenkins assured Chen that Al would not betray them, Chen decided to leave anyway. In the middle of the night, he hiked to the main road and walked back to the nearest town. In town, he left an anonymous note at the local police station tipping them off about the location of the kidnapped boy. The note soon led to the boy's safe return. Putting aside conspiracy charges, can Al be found responsible for the kidnapping as a party to the crime?

A. No. Al withdrew before the crime was ever committed.

B. No. Al never involved himself in the crime.

C. Yes. Al never effectively withdrew from the enterprise.

D. Yes. Once engaged in the enterprise, Al could not withdraw without any liability.

42. Will Chen be found responsible?

ANSWER:

43. Angelica and Stefano are both college students pursuing degrees in business. Nervous about a big economics exam, Angelica suggested they break into their professor's office to steal a copy of the exam before test day. Stefano originally agreed because he was worried about his grade in the class, but on the day of the planned theft, he got cold feet. Instead of breaking into the office with Angelica, Stefano said he would wait outside the building and be on the lookout for anyone entering. Stefano no longer wanted to be involved in the plan, but he did not want to upset Angelica. If Angelica is caught, will Stefano be liable even though he did not break into the office with her?

A. Yes, Stefano is still liable under an accomplice theory of liability because of his involvement as a lookout.

B. Yes, Stefano is still liable because he intended to be the lookout.

C. No, Stefano is not liable because he no longer intended to be involved in the theft.

D. No, Stefano is not liable because he withdrew from the crime.

44. Joanna is a government official charged with soliciting bids for the construction of her community's new high school. Gerald, a construction company tycoon, bribed Joanna with a large discount on the construction of her own new house. Ultimately, Gerald's construction company was awarded the contract for the new high school. After the bribe was discovered, Gerald was charged with giving the bribe and Joanna was charged with receiving the bribe. Joanna was acquitted of the charge because the court found that she did not know she had received such a substantial discount on her home construction. In a separate and subsequent trial, Gerald was convicted of giving the bribe. Gerald considered this result unfair given Joanna's acquittal. He appealed on the ground that his conviction could not stand when Joanna was acquitted of receiving the bribe Gerald allegedly gave. Will he win this argument?

ANSWER:

The Inchoate Offenses

SOLICITATION

45. Peter and Kiara were talking at a neighborhood barbeque, and Peter began discussing his marital problems. Kiara commented that Peter would be better off without his wife, and that if his wife were out of the picture, perhaps Kiara and Peter could get together. It appeared that Peter took this comment seriously, mentioning to Kiara later that night some possible methods of eliminating his wife. After several weeks, Peter's behavior grew increasingly odd, and he talked about the earlier conversation at the party several times. Kiara became concerned that he was giving genuine consideration to killing his wife. Kiara approached him to tell him she was only joking at the party, but Peter brushed off her concerns. Several days later, Peter attempted to kill his wife. Is Kiara guilty of solicitation?

ANSWER:

46. If the evidence in the problem above is not sufficient to prove solicitation, which of these additional items of evidence would be most helpful to the government in persuading the trier of fact that a solicitation was committed by Kiara:

A. Kiara posted an entry on her *Facebook* page in which she recited a poem with the theme of, "I hope he does it, she deserves it." She never identified the "he" or "she" in the poem.

B. Kiara wrote an e-mail message to Peter saying, "your wife sure is a creep, she deserves whatever punishment she gets."

C. In a phone message, Kiara said, "I know you are having problems with your car, feel free to use mine to finish up any serious family business you might have."

D. All of the above.

47. Miguel and Steven were two college students eating lunch in the cafeteria. Their conversation was cut short when Carter, a hulking brute, began taunting a student at the next table about her clothing. Steven said to Miguel, "Somebody ought to give that guy what he deserves." Several days later, Miguel slashed Carter's tires. Is Steven guilty of the crime of solicitation?

    A. Yes, because Steven was the creative force behind the crime.

    B. Yes, because Steven encouraged Miguel to commit the crime.

    C. No, because Miguel was the only one to commit an affirmative act toward the crime.

    D. No, because Steven did not intend for Miguel to slash Carter's tires.

48. On several occasions, Hanh heard the new waiter at the restaurant where she worked talk about "doing drugs." She approached him and asked if he knew where she could obtain some cocaine. He responded that he wasn't sure, but he could ask around. Hanh thanked him and gave him some cash, saying, "This should cover the cost if you happen to locate any for me. If you can't find any, just give me the cash back. I'm sure you're good for it." However, the new waiter was actually a police officer conducting an undercover investigation of the restaurant's owners and would never have aided her. Can Hanh be convicted of solicitation?

    A. Yes, because the person approached need not accept the request for the crime of solicitation to be complete.

    B. Yes, because the person involved was a police officer.

    C. No, because the police officer would have never accepted her request for assistance.

    D. No, because Hanh did not manifest the state of mind of intent by simply asking a question.

49. Tony was in the hospital recovering from a recent fight with his neighbor, Pete. He and Pete have had many serious fights in the past, but this time, Tony sustained major injuries because Pete hit him with a baseball bat. Tony wrote a letter to a friend, asking him to find Pete and inflict "a big time hurt" upon him. Tony gave the letter to a nurse to be mailed, but the nurse left it lying on a table near the nurses' station. Later, Pete came over to visit Tony and to apologize about their previous altercation. Pete noticed the letter and grew suspicious that Tony was writing to his friend following the fight. Pete opened the letter and discovered Tony's proposal to have him attacked. Pete took the letter to the police. Can Tony be found guilty of solicitation?

A. No, the letter never got to his friend, so he could not be guilty of soliciting a crime.

B. No, Tony's letter only reflected a natural impulsive reaction to his situation and would not constitute a solicitation to commit a crime.

C. Yes, the crime of solicitation was complete when Tony wrote the letter.

D. Yes, as long as Tony intended that the crime take place and made some effort to effectuate that intent.

50. Two police officers were monitoring a street in a neighborhood with high drug and crime rates. They observed a man standing in the middle of the street, dressed oddly and holding a sign that said, "I sell pies." There were no baked goods visible near the man. Suspicious that he might be selling illegal drugs, the two officers observed him for some time and noticed several cars stopping near the man. The man leaned into each car and spoke to each driver. Each car drove off and made the same left turn at the next stoplight. The two cops drove around the block and back toward the man. When they rolled down the window the man became agitated and said, "I'm just trying to sell my stuff!" Assuming the police are unable to find out where the cars went after stopping by the man with the pie sign, can the man be successfully prosecuted for solicitation to purchase illegal drugs?

A. No. There is no direct evidence that a crime was being solicited.

B. No. If the officers did not hear the conversations between the man and the drivers, the government will not be able to establish intent.

C. Yes. Circumstantial evidence can establish that the man was attempting to stop people for the purpose of giving them information about where to purchase illegal drugs. The man's failure to have any pastry goods in sight serves to show that he was in fact trying to solicit illegal drug purchasers and not pie purchasers.

D. Yes. The man's odd dress, suspicious location, unusual claim to be selling pies, and the similar driving pattern of all the cars that stopped could establish that he was engaged in soliciting people to purchase illegal drugs.

51. Brigid and Camille were at a party when Brigid's ex-boyfriend Adam walked in. Brigid confided in Camille that Adam mistreated her and broke her heart. By the end of the night, both women have had a good time at the party and were feeling intoxicated. As they exited the party, Brigid made a comment to Camille wishing someone would "put Adam in his place," and the two discussed ways they would "teach Adam a lesson," including damaging his car, which Brigid pointed out to Camille. The next morning, Brigid saw on social media that Adam's car was stolen and then crashed a few blocks away from the party. If Camille is responsible, can Brigid be successfully charged with solicitation?

A. Yes, Brigid can be charged with solicitation for encouraging Camille to "teach Adam a lesson," and providing her with ideas of how to do so.

B. Yes, Brigid can be charged with solicitation because she told Camille Adam mistreated her and gave Camille a motive to target Adam.

C. No, Brigid will not be successfully charged with solicitation because both she and Camille were intoxicated when they had the conversation about Adam.

D. No, Brigid did not specifically tell Camille to crash Adam's car, so she cannot be found liable for solicitation.

E. No, Brigid and Camille were both intoxicated and Brigid did not ask Camille to specifically damage Adam's car.

ATTEMPT

52. found out, through the use of a private investigator, that her husband had been having an affair with Katia, Sally's best friend since childhood. Furious with Katia and her husband, Sally decided to get back at both of them. Her plan was to tamper with her husband's car before he left work to go "bowling" (which, she had found out, was actually his cover-up for the times he went with Katia to a local motel). Sally's idea was that he and Katia would be involved in a fiery car crash. However, Sally knew nothing about cars. In order to prepare for her plan, she took a basic auto class through the local community college. She did not tell her husband about the class. One day she returned from class and found her husband holding up a tuition bill and a bill for the private investigator. Sally dissolved into tears and told him that she knew about the affair; she also told him about her plans to kill him and Katia. Sally's husband recorded the entire conversation and turned the recording in to the police, along with the two bills. Can Sally be found guilty of attempted murder?

A. No. It is not clear that Sally really intended to murder her husband and Katia.

B. No. Sally had not yet completed the auto class and had plenty of time left to change her mind.

C. Yes. Sally had taken a substantial step toward her plan to kill the two by enrolling in the auto class.

D. Yes. Sally had a plan and took action by taking the auto class. In addition, there is no evidence to suggest that she would have aborted the plan if her husband had not confronted her with the two bills.

53. Suppose Sally's plan had not been discovered initially by her husband. Instead, just before she was able to tamper with the car, the police found her waiting to act, in the parking lot of the husband's office. She did not tell the police of her plan, but her husband figured this out, told the authorities and gave them the information about the auto shop class and the private investigator. Now can Sally be found guilty of attempted murder?

ANSWER:

54. Sally, on her way home from finding out from the private investigator that her husband was having an affair, was so upset that she ran a red light going 75 MPH in a 25 MPH speed zone. By pure coincidence, the car she crashed into was her husband's car. He was severely injured, but ultimately made a miraculous recovery. Can Sally be convicted of the crime of attempted murder?

A. No. Running a red light, even at such a high speed, is not reckless enough for a conviction of either murder or the attempt offense.

B. No. Sally lacks the requisite *mens rea* for the charge.

C. Yes. Sally's actions would have constituted murder had her husband died from his injuries.

D. Yes. Sally must have subconsciously intended to hit her husband, so the intent required for attempt is met.

55. Doug decided to rob a bank. He planned the heist for several weeks and rented an apartment near the bank where he believed he could avoid detection for a few months before moving to a new city. He set a date for the robbery and found an accomplice who could break into the safe, but he had no clearly established plans yet for the details of the robbery. It turned out that this accomplice, the supposed expert on safe cracking, was actually an undercover police officer, and Doug was immediately arrested for attempted armed robbery. Doug confessed to the plan. Can Doug be convicted of this crime without any other evidence?

ANSWER:

56. Julia broke into the home of her neighbor, an old enemy, and was going to shoot him while he was sleeping. Julia was unaware that her husband had earlier unloaded her gun, for fear that she would do something rash and kill someone. The neighbor awoke and screamed when he saw an intruder, so Julia ran out of his house. Can Julia be convicted of attempted murder even though the gun was unloaded?

   A. Yes, the fact that the gun was unloaded does not preclude a conviction of attempt.

   B. Yes, because Julia broke into the neighbor's house, she must have meant to kill him.

   C. No, because Julia may have only wanted to scare the neighbor.

   D. No, because there was no way under these circumstances that Julia could have killed the victim.

57. In the problem above, could Julia be convicted of attempted murder if the neighbor was not actually at home when Julia broke into the house?

   A. Yes, any action taken in furtherance of a planned crime constitutes an attempt.

   B. Yes, if Julia thought the neighbor was home when she broke in.

   C. No, it would have been impossible for Julia to shoot the neighbor that night.

   D. No, Julia's crime here was burglary, not attempted murder.

58. Yolanda had been caring for her elderly aunt for some months now, hoping to eventually recover a large portion of her aunt's considerable estate. Growing impatient with her situation and eager to collect under her aunt's will as soon as possible, Yolanda replaced her aunt's vitamins with lethal poison. When her aunt remained unaffected by the new pills, Yolanda learned that she had given the aunt a harmless herbal supplement rather than the lethal drug. Feeling remorseful about her evil motives, Yolanda then decided to just wait for her aunt's natural end. Has she committed attempted murder?

   A. Yes, because society has an interest in punishing people's bad thoughts.

   B. Yes, because Yolanda had the intent to kill her aunt and took a substantial act toward the commission of the crime.

   C. No, because Yolanda's decision not to go through with her plan precludes prosecution for attempted murder.

   D. No, because there is no way the herbal supplement could have been lethal.

CONSPIRACY

59. Sybil and John agreed to kidnap the daughter of a local politician and hold her for ransom. Their plan succeeded, and they released the child after receiving the money. They were apprehended several days later. Under the majority rule, can each of them be convicted of — and sentenced for — both kidnapping and conspiracy to commit the kidnapping?

    A. Yes, because conspiracy does not merge with the completed offense, so convictions for both the completed offense and conspiracy to commit that offense would be allowed.

    B. No. Because the conspiracy and the kidnapping share the same objectives, merger of the two offenses is required.

    C. No. As with the other inchoate offenses of solicitation and attempt, conspiracy merges with the completed offense if the completed offense is a felony.

    D. No, because the common law rule dictates that one act cannot result in more than one punishment.

60. In the above problem, would sentencing Sybil and John for both kidnapping and conspiracy violate the constitution?

61. Say that Sybil and John had a third partner, Gertie, involved in the kidnapping. Gertie helped coordinate the logistics of the kidnapping, and it was her idea to target this specific politician. Before Sybil and John took the child, Gertie was arrested for her involvement and put in jail. Can Gertie still be convicted of conspiracy for the subsequent kidnapping and ransom request?

ANSWER:

62. Erika and Lauren went into a convenience store to buy some sodas and snacks. When they entered the store, they browsed the aisles a bit and noticed that no one was attending the cash register. Erika went behind the counter and started trying to open the cash register. Erika exchanged brief eye contact with her friend. Lauren said nothing, but giggled a bit and looked around nervously. Erika managed to get the cash register open, filled her pockets with the cash, and started running out of the store with Lauren. The two young women were in the parking lot when the owner of the shop came from the back room, realized what had occurred, and telephoned the police. Erika and Lauren were caught several minutes later. Can they be convicted of conspiracy to commit theft?

A. Yes, because there was an explicit agreement to commit the crime.

B. Yes, because there was an implied understanding, and no explicit agreement is required for a conspiracy.

C. No, because there was no explicit agreement to commit the crime.

D. No, because Lauren did not do anything to suggest she was in agreement.

63. Kate and her sister Emily were not on the best of terms. At their cousin's wedding, Kate's sister humiliated her in front of their entire family. Kate sat outside the party thinking about how to get back at her sister when Emily's husband Thomas approached her. Kate and Thomas talked for hours, discussing Emily's malevolent nature. Finally, Thomas suggested that Kate should hire someone to really hurt and scare Emily. He said it would teach Emily a lesson, Kate would feel vindicated, and the sisters would finally be able to put the past behind them. Kate would have to take the lead role because, Thomas explained, he and Emily had been having so many marital problems that he would immediately be under suspicion. He said he would, however, be happy to do much of the planning. Kate was shocked to hear her brother-in-law suggest such a thing and she said nothing. Thomas continued to elaborate on his proposal, and Kate said she agreed to the plan, although in reality she never would consider harming Emily in such a way. Over the next few days, Thomas discussed with Kate having Emily "roughed up" by someone because she had made everybody's life so miserable. Uncertain of how to proceed, Kate called the police to tell them of Thomas' plans. The police instructed Kate to act as if she planned to carry out the crime. Thomas talked about making arrangements for Emily's beating. When he met with Kate to instruct her how to contact "the thug" he had located, their conversation was covertly recorded and Thomas was soon arrested. According to the common law approach, can Thomas be convicted of a conspiracy offense?

    A. Yes, because Thomas believed himself to be acting pursuant to an agreement with Kate.

    B. Yes, because there was an agreement by Thomas and Kate to have Emily beaten.

    C. No, because Kate never intended to carry out the agreement, there was no true agreement.

    D. No, because without Kate's agreement and subsequent actions, Thomas could not carry out his plan.

64. In the previous question, of what crime would Thomas be guilty?

65. Would the answer to Question 63 change under the modern trend?

66. Joel, an undercover drug agent, visited the apartment of Betty, a reputed drug dealer. Betty agreed to sell Joel a quantity of drugs; she divided his portion from a large amount she had on hand. Unable to find a container for it, she called her boyfriend Zeb, and asked if he had any plastic bags. From the bedroom, Zeb responded that she could find some bags in the kitchen pantry. Betty located the bags and completed the sale to Joel. Betty was convicted of distribution of an illegal substance. Under the majority rule, could her deal with Joel give rise to a conspiracy conviction for Betty?

   A. Yes, because Betty satisfied the requirements of intent, agreement and action in furtherance of that agreement.

   B. No, because Joel was an undercover officer and therefore was not really intending to buy the drugs.

   C. No, because Betty has already been convicted of the substantive offense of distribution.

   D. No, because Joel's actions here constitute entrapment, providing Betty a complete defense.

67. Under the facts above, could Zeb be convicted of conspiracy?

   ANSWER:

68. Reggie often hung out on the street in front of Karry's convenience store. Reggie occasionally came in for purchases when he had some money. One night, he came in with a group of teenagers and bought a large quantity of beer. He began to come in with the kids every week or so. Karry received a notice from the alcohol regulatory board that underage purchasers might be buying alcohol through other purchasers, pointing out that kids had been approaching people with a little money to entice them into purchasing alcohol on their behalf. For the next few weeks, Reggie came in every few days and bought a large quantity of beer, each time with the teenagers next to him. One day, an undercover police officer was in the store, and after questioning the group, he determined that Reggie was purchasing alcohol for the teenagers. While Karry's license to sell alcoholic beverages will certainly be reviewed, could she also face criminal liability for conspiracy?

   A. No, because there is no evidence that Karry had an agreement with Reggie.

   B. No, because Karry committed no crime in selling the alcohol to Reggie, as he is of legal age.

   C. No, because the crime of conspiracy requires a criminal intent.

   D. Yes, because an agreement to commit a crime could be inferred from her relationship with Reggie.

69. Eddie was leaving a concert one night when he saw Marco, a guy who owed him money. Eddie said to his friends, "Hey, we gotta get that guy," and he and his friends chased Marco down and attacked him. The group forced Marco to the ground, punching and kicking him and yelling that he'd better pay Eddie. Marco tried to run away from his attackers. Confused and disoriented, he ran into the street without looking. Marco was hit by a car and died several hours later at the hospital. Can Eddie and his friends be convicted of conspiracy to commit murder?

   A. Yes, because their intent and agreement to attack Marco are clear from their actions.

   B. Yes, because their behavior demonstrates their actions as reckless, allowing a conviction of murder as well as a conviction of conspiracy to commit murder.

   C. No, it is not clear that Eddie's group agreed to any plan, so they cannot be held responsible for conspiracy.

   D. No, because they did not demonstrate the necessary intent to carry out the crime of conspiracy to commit murder.

70. Would the result in the above problem change if Eddie and his friends were charged with conspiracy to commit battery?

71. Catherine and Steve supplemented their income while in college by distributing methamphetamine. Their operation was fairly small-scale. Steve usually purchased a quantity from a dealer in a nearby town, although Catherine provided the original contact, and the couple sold mostly to students they knew. When Steve began using drugs heavily, their relationship went sour, and they split apart. Catherine graduated from college with honors and worked for three years at a consulting firm. Never telling Steve her plans, she had no significant contact with Steve during the three-year period, and was eager to put that earlier period of her life behind her, staying clear of the drug scene entirely. Steve's path was much different. He found himself deeply in debt shortly after Catherine left and he began increasing his operations in order to pay back his creditors and supplement his own drug habit. After Catherine left, Steve found a few other individuals to work with in the operation. Unfortunately for Steve, one of those people was an undercover police officer. If Steve and his circle of contacts in the drug world are convicted of conspiracy to distribute illegal substances, could Catherine also be convicted of that crime?

   A. Yes, because Catherine took part in the criminal enterprise from the beginning and would be responsible for all later actions.

   B. Yes, because the foreseeable actions of one conspirator can be attributed to another.

   C. No, because Steve's actions were unforeseeable.

   D. No, because Catherine had distanced herself from the operation for some time.

72. In the fact pattern above, assume that before she left him, Catherine tried to help Steve get out of the drug business and go to a rehabilitation center. She even told him of her plans. She also contacted the school and police officials anonymously to inform them of Steve's conduct. In most jurisdictions, would this absolve her of liability for the later criminal acts?

    A. Yes, because Catherine withdrew from the criminal enterprise.

    B. Yes, because she made it clear that her role in the scheme was over.

    C. No, because the crime of conspiracy was already complete.

    D. No, because she was an essential part of the conspiracy at its inception.

73. What if, at the time of Steve's prosecution, Catherine had been uninvolved for three and a half years. The statute of limitations on the conspiracy charge is three years. Can Catherine still be successfully prosecuted?

    A. Yes, because the crime had not been discovered until after the statute of limitations had run.

    B. Yes, because the conspiracy continued to operate, so the statute of limitations had not begun to run.

    C. No, because one cannot be charged with a crime for actions taken after the statute of limitations has run.

    D. No, because she had not been involved and therefore cannot be charged for the crimes of others.

74. Cooper and Jalen were two prisoners who shared a common dislike for their fellow prisoner, Sheldon. One day, in the cafeteria, Jalen noticed Cooper backing Sheldon into a corner and threatening him. Cooper and Sheldon began to argue, and Sheldon punched Cooper in the stomach. Jalen ran over to the fight. Jalen and Cooper both started punching and kicking Sheldon. Suddenly, Cooper pulled out a rudimentary knife he had made and stabbed Sheldon twice. Jalen merely stood there as the stabbing occurred. Can Jalen be successfully charged with the crime of conspiracy to commit murder if Sheldon dies? The crime of murder?

ANSWER:

75. Cary and Allen decided to enter the interstate drug trafficking business. They would receive drugs at a designated location along the main north-south interstate up and down the coast and then transport them, for sale, to another designated location further along on the interstate. The two bought a van and rented apartments near the drop-off and pick-up locations. Before actually receiving the first shipment of drugs, local authorities were tipped off and the two were arrested and charged with a violation of a federal conspiracy statute. Can they be convicted of being involved in two conspiracies, conspiracy to possess and conspiracy to distribute, under the same conspiracy statute?

   A. Yes. Cary and Allen agreed to two distinct criminal acts.

   B. Yes. Conspiracy may be broken into separate crimes when linked with distinct statutes and when their actions have been successful.

   C. No. Buying a van and renting the apartments are acts too insubstantial in furtherance of the plot to qualify under the conspiracy statute.

   D. No. A single agreement cannot be broken into separate conspiracy charges under one general conspiracy statute.

76. Would the answer change if Cary and Allen were prosecuted under two separate conspiracy statutes, one dealing with possession and the other dealing with distribution?

   A. Yes, because the government would have shown two separate and distinct agreements.

   B. Yes, as two separate conspiracy statutes would demonstrate the legislature's intent that one agreement could be broken into separate conspiracy prosecutions.

   C. No. One agreement can only be the basis for one conspiracy prosecution.

   D. No. Such a prosecution would violate double jeopardy principles.

Crimes

THE PROPERTY OFFENSES: LARCENY, EMBEZZLEMENT, FALSE PRETENSES

77. While shopping one day, Rodrigo came across a black leather jacket that he just had to have. Unfortunately, it was out of his price range. Rodrigo slipped off his own inexpensive coat and put on the jacket. He went into the dressing room to try it on, where he also stopped to rip off the security sensor and the price tag. He continued to browse through the shop and made his way toward the exit, looking around him to be sure that nobody was observing him. A few steps out on the street, Rodrigo was stopped by a security guard. He was subsequently arrested for larceny. Has Rodrigo committed larceny?

    A. Yes, because he intended to steal the jacket and left the premises.

    B. No, because he intended to steal, but was unsuccessful.

    C. No, because he was not trespassing.

    D. No, because although he left the store, he was still in the vicinity of it.

78. Juanita was the manager of a flower store. As such, she had full responsibility for ordering and pricing goods, hiring and firing employees, and promoting the store generally. One day she took home a fancy plant, sold it to her friend, and kept the money. What crime has she committed?

    A. Embezzlement.

    B. Larceny.

    C. False pretenses.

    D. Robbery.

79. Amy was visiting one of her favorite cities. She went to dinner at a famed restaurant and enjoyed an extravagant, four-course meal, complete with a bottle of very expensive wine. When the hefty check came, she reached into her purse and realized she had forgotten her wallet back in her hotel room. She panicked and decided that the meal would have been more than she could afford anyway. She gathered her things, headed for the restroom, and exited out a service entrance, never paying her bill. Has Amy committed larceny?

ANSWER:

80. Thomas worked for a large bank managing trusts for wealthy clients. He personally invested his money conservatively and did not often buy large quantities of stock. Marta, a friend from college, called him one afternoon and talked with him at length about a young biotech company for which Marta worked. She mentioned some things about this company that convinced Thomas that it would be incredibly profitable within five years. Thomas also learned from another source that this company was about to have a public offering. Unfortunately, Thomas's personal assets were not "liquid," and by the time he would be able to raise enough capital, the opportunity to invest would be lost. Thomas decided to skew the numbers at work a bit and "borrow" some cash from the bank in order to purchase shares in this company. He knew he could return the money within a short time if all went well. If Thomas's dealings came to light some time later, could he be found guilty of embezzlement?

- **A.** Yes, even if Thomas were able to return the money, he still embezzled from the company.

- **B.** Yes, but if Thomas actually returned the money before he was caught, he will not be convicted.

- **C.** No, because Thomas was not acting as an employee at the time.

- **D.** No, if he returned the funds, subsequently, he would not be found guilty because he was only temporarily borrowing the money.

81. Luis' job involved marketing corporate contracts for a national cellular communications company. In the course of his job, he often provided free phones and discounted service, on a discretionary basis, to important people working for his corporate clients. As such, he usually had many expensive, advanced mobile phones in his possession and the ability to provide service discounts, with very little oversight from supervisors of the telecommunications company. As a favor to a personal friend, Luis gave her a new phone for free and provided her with discounted service. When his supervisor discovered this favor, Luis was fired. Can Luis be found guilty of embezzlement?

- **A.** No. He did not intend to embezzle from the company.

- **B.** No. He was merely providing equipment to people, not taking money.

C. Yes. The statute likely encompasses the taking or conversion of property as well as money.

D. Yes. His company fired him for abusing his discretion.

82. Pamela and Michael hired Chris to build their dream home. After discussing the details, all parties signed a contract, and Pamela and Michael paid Chris an initial down payment of $25,000. While the contract did not specify what the money would be used for, Pamela and Michael assumed Chris would put it towards construction costs. Chris never finished constructing their home and never contacted Pamela and Michael again. Pamela and Michael later found out that Chris had done the same thing to four other couples he was contracted to work with in the past. Is Chris guilty of embezzlement?

A. Yes, because Chris intended to deprive Pamela and Michael of their money permanently.

B. Yes, because Chris did not fulfill the contract, so he was required to return the remainder of the down payment.

C. No, because the $25,000 belonged to Chris after he received it.

D. No, because Chris originally intended to complete the project.

83. While out for a walk in his neighborhood Lawrence noticed a car that was up for sale. Lawrence called the number listed on the side of the car and told the car's owner, Teri, that he was interested in buying the car. He said that as a mechanic and avid car enthusiast, Lawrence knew the car was not worth the $20,000 selling price. Instead, Lawrence said he would be willing to pay only $15,000, which he reiterated was the true value of the car based on his knowledge and experience. Teri was eager to sell the car and did not know much about cars herself. She agreed to the $15,000 payment and agreed to meet Lawrence on the upcoming Friday to make the exchange. On Friday, Lawrence handed Teri a $15,000 check and received the keys to the vehicle. It was not until later that evening, during a conversation with her father, when Teri realized that her old car was actually worth double the amount that she sold it for. Teri attempted to contact Lawrence but the number she had was no longer in service. To make matters worse, Teri was extremely embarrassed when the $15,000 check bounced after she tried to deposit it at the bank. Can Lawrence be found guilty of false pretenses?

A. Yes, because Lawrence misrepresented his profession and knowledge of cars.

B. Yes, because Lawrence lied about the price of the car and knowingly gave Teri a bad check.

C. No, because Teri accepted Lawrence's $15,000 offer.

D. No, because Lawrence could not foresee that the check would bounce.

84. Daniel, a college sophomore, needed money to pay his school's tuition fees. While scrolling on Instagram, Daniel saw someone post that they were willing to pay $1,000 for a specific pair of sneakers. Daniel responded to the post and said that he had a pair of the sneakers and was interested in selling them. Desperate, Daniel bought a pair of plain white sneakers and "customized" them to match the sneakers the buyer was looking for. The following week, Daniel and the buyer met and made the exchange. One hour later, the buyer noticed that a logo present on the real sneakers was missing from the sneakers Daniel sold him. The buyer attempted to reach Daniel and get his money back, but Daniel had since deleted his social media accounts. Can Daniel be found guilty of obtaining money by false pretenses?

    A. Yes, because Daniel intentionally passed the shoes off as being authentic.

    B. Yes, because Daniel knew that the buyer would believe that the shoes were authentic.

    C. No, because the buyer never questioned the authenticity of the shoes.

    D. No, because the buyer realized the shoes were not authentic too late.

85. After being unemployed for a couple of months, Stephanie was ready to take almost any employment she could find. Sitting at a neighborhood bar one evening, another patron named Gary told her about a great money-making opportunity if Stephanie would help him set up a new business. All that was required was for Stephanie to call potential investors to see if they would be interested in establishing a new retirement community on the edge of town. As Gary explained it to Stephanie, the development would be run like a condominium, with all of the residents being involved from the earliest stages of the project, in order to maximize each person's retirement dreams. Once a threshold of investors was brought in, decisions on planning and amenities could be decided by the investors themselves, so they could actually shape their future community. Stephanie thought this sounded like a great idea and she wanted a job. She called area seniors with this exact information given to her by Gary, indicating that the property had been purchased and preliminary roads put in, but the remainder of the project depended on individual contributions. Stephanie raised thousands of dollars within a couple of weeks and was paid handsomely for her success. An investigation by area law enforcement revealed that Gary had purchased no land in the area and was merely taking the money from the project's investors. Can Stephanie now be found guilty of false presences?

    A. Yes, because Stephanie misrepresented to her clients a material fact.

    B. Yes, because Stephanie was involved in a criminal operation to defraud area seniors.

    C. No, because Stephanie did not have knowledge that the representations were false.

    D. No, because if there was a misrepresentation, it was of a future fact (i.e., that the community would be built), not of a past or present fact.

OFFENSES AGAINST THE HABITATION: BURGLARY, ARSON

86. Sara was at home and turned on the TV to watch a program at 8:00 p.m. She heard someone on her porch. Thinking it was her boyfriend, she unlocked the front door. On her porch was a strange man who demanded that she let him in the house. When she refused, he pulled out a knife. Sara, fearful for her life, let him in. Once inside, he searched the house for valuables, took her engagement ring and cash from a drawer, and then left the house. Under the common law definition, has this man committed burglary?

    A. Yes, because he constructively met all of the requirements for burglary.

    B. Yes, because he robbed her in her home.

    C. No, because he did not commit a breaking to gain entry.

    D. No, because the crime occurred early in the evening.

87. What would result if the incident took place at 8:00 a.m. rather than 8:00 p.m.?

    A. Same result at common law.

    B. Different result at common law.

    C. Same result under the modern statutes.

    D. Different result under the modern statutes.

88. Alicia and Bella were married and were happy for a time. Thereafter, however, their relationship collapsed and Bella moved out of their house. They still co-owned the house. Alicia changed the locks on the house and Bella no longer came around the neighborhood. One year later, Bella went to the house and "jimmied" the front door lock one night while Alicia was away; Bella entered and proceeded to trash the inside of the house. Can Bella be convicted of burglary?

ANSWER:

89. Dave was drunk and decided to sober up by taking a drive. On his way out of town, Dave flung his lit cigarette butt out the window of his vehicle. The cigarette caused a fire that destroyed several homes. The fire was finally put out by a heavy rain later. Can Dave be convicted of arson?

ANSWER:

90. Nicolena was extremely envious of her next door neighbor. Plotting to burn down the neighbor's house (so that he would move away), Nicolena planted an explosive device on the wall of the neighbor's home. The plan was that the device would explode, and the house would then catch fire and burn down. The device was set off and it did explode. It caused extensive damage, but it did not actually cause anything to catch fire. Can Nicolena be found guilty of arson?

   A. Yes, Nicolena intentionally damaged the house.

   B. No, Nicolena never entered the neighbor's house.

   C. No, arson can be found only if the residence is entirely destroyed.

   D. No, arson can be found only if some part of the residence catches fire.

91. In the above problem, what crime did Nicolena commit?

   ANSWER:

HOMICIDE

Killing

92. Sam hated Keesha because she was more popular than he was. One evening, he grabbed Keesha outside her house and threw her into his car. Sam drove to a remote location and shot Keesha. Amazingly, Keesha was found alive and taken to a hospital. Keesha lay in a coma as a result of the gunshot and died 395 days later. Under the common law, is Sam guilty of murder?

   A. Yes, because Sam had the intent to kill Keesha and she died as a result of his actions.

   B. No, because Keesha died too long after she was shot.

   C. No, because Sam only wanted to hurt Keesha, not kill her; he hoped that someone would find her.

   D. No, because Sam was clearly crazy; a sane person would not shoot another person in this situation.

93. What result in the above problem today in most states?

   ANSWER:

94. Jane snuck into John's house in the middle of the night and shot him twice while he appeared to be sleeping. Unbeknownst to Jane, John was already dead because Fritz had put poison in John's wine at dinner earlier that night. Is Jane guilty of murder since she had the intent to kill John and she actually shot him?

    A. No, because Jane did not cause John's death.

    B. No, because Jane's actions might not have killed John if he had been alive.

    C. Yes, because Jane had the intent to kill John and committed the act.

    D. Yes, because Jane should be punished for her actions that would have resulted in death if John had been alive.

95. In the above problem, what crime did Jane commit?

    ANSWER:

96. Marie told William she was pregnant with his child. William was not pleased and decided to leave town. Five months later, William returned and attacked Marie. William punched Marie in the abdomen several times, saying he hoped the baby would die. Marie immediately went into premature labor and gave birth to a girl. In order to convict William of murder under the common law, does it matter if the baby was born alive and died minutes later, or if she was stillborn?

    A. No. In both cases William had the intent to kill and committed the act resulting in the baby's death.

    B. No. William cannot be found guilty of murder in either case because the act in both cases was committed before the baby's birth.

    C. No. In both cases there may have been other reasons why the baby died.

    D. Yes. A baby must be born alive for a defendant to be found guilty of murder, which involves the killing of a person.

97. Would your previous answer be different in states that have enacted feticide statutes?

    ANSWER:

98. James was seriously injured in a car accident when the drunk driver of another car recklessly swerved into his lane. After being transported to the hospital, James's heart was still beating. Nonetheless, he was connected to a respirator, was being tube-fed, and exhibited no reflexes or brain stem activity. If the doctors disconnect him from life-support, is the driver of the car that hit James guilty of a homicide offense under modern statutes?

    A. No, because James's heart was beating at the time of the doctors' actions.

    B. No, because the doctors killed James when they turned off the life support.

    C. Yes, because James was brain dead.

    D. No, because a homicide offense cannot be based on a car accident.

MURDER

99. Amy and Bess were good friends until Bess "stole" Amy's boyfriend Bernardo a month ago. Amy wanted to "remove Bess from the picture." Amy saw Bess at the mall and talked things over with her. Amy said she forgave Bess for going out with Bernardo. Friends once again, they went out driving together. Amy began speeding down the road, shouting with exhilaration into the wind. Amy wrapped her car around a telephone pole while driving at speeds in excess of 130 mph. Bess was killed in the crash. Is Amy guilty of murder?

    A. Yes, because driving at such high speeds shows a complete disregard for the safety of others.

    B. Yes, because Amy previously had the intent to kill Bess.

    C. No, because Bess voluntarily got in the car with Amy.

    D. No, because Amy was having fun and did not stop to think that they might be in an accident.

100. Jolinda had severe muscular dystrophy. Michael was a nurse paid through a trust fund to take care of Jolinda. Authorities recently found Jolinda in an appalling condition. She appeared emaciated, with sores from lying in bed for several weeks straight. Although the police took Jolinda straight to the hospital, she could not be saved and died a few days later from malnutrition. Under the common law, would Michael be guilty of murder?

    A. No, because he had no duty to act.

    B. No, because he did not commit any act that resulted in Jolinda's death.

    C. Yes, because he was obligated to take care of Jolinda and failed to do so.

    D. Yes, because the law punishes any person for allowing another human to live in such a condition.

101. Leonard's upstairs neighbor was a grumpy woman with a serious heart condition. She called the police whenever Leonard had a party and yelled that his television was too loud. She also reported him to the landlord for propping open the outer door to the apartment building. Leonard could not stand his neighbor and devised a plan to get rid of her permanently.

First, Leonard appeared to befriend his elderly neighbor. He began offering to carry her groceries up the stairs and he spoke to her politely. He even kept his television volume turned down. He knew that the woman's daughter came by every Sunday promptly at 2:00 p.m. One Sunday, he caught the woman's daughter entering the building and told her that her mother wanted her to pick up a few items at the store. When he handed her a list, the daughter left the building. After waiting a short time, Leonard went to the woman's apartment. She told him that she was worried because her daughter was never late. He responded that "the police just came 'round. Your daughter was in a car accident on the way here; she's dead. I told them you should hear this from a friend." The old woman sank to the floor, crying. Then she clutched her chest and gasped for breath. Pleased that his plan worked so well, Leonard stood and watched as she died. Is Leonard guilty of murder?

ANSWER:

102. Abdul and Eric had never met before, but they were in the same cafe when a brawl started. Caught up in the mayhem, Abdul swung wildly and punched Eric in the face. Eric died from the injuries. Is Abdul guilty of murder?

A. No, because Abdul did not intend to kill Eric.

B. No, because Abdul did not have the necessary state of mind for murder.

C. Yes, because Abdul intended to inflict serious bodily injury on Eric.

D. Yes, because Abdul acted recklessly.

103. In the problem above, suppose that Abdul was a giant of a man, 6'5" tall, weighing about 300 pounds and was a former professional fighter. Would the result be different?

ANSWER:

104. Arturo went into a high school and took an unattended backpack. As he was slowly driving his car out of the school parking lot, he accidentally hit and killed a student who ran out from behind a parked car. Is Arturo guilty of murder?

A. No, because Arturo did not intend to hit the student.

B. No, because larceny of a backpack is not an inherently dangerous felony.

C. Yes, because Arturo killed the student while leaving a crime scene.

D. Yes, because Arturo could not have hit a student without being grossly reckless.

105. Would Arturo be guilty of murder if, instead of stealing an unattended backpack, he took the backpack from its owner at gunpoint before accidentally hitting the student while driving away?

A. No, because it was an accident.

B. No, because the robbery was completed prior to killing the student.

C. Yes, because the student was killed during the commission of a violent felony.

D. Yes, because the student died as a result of being hit by the thief's car.

106. Matt fled the scene after committing an armed robbery. As he ran down an alley, a policeman aimed his gun at Matt and fired. The policeman's bullet accidentally killed an innocent bystander. Is Matt liable for the homicide under a felony murder theory?

ANSWER:

107. Suppose Matt, while trying to escape, took a hostage and used him as a shield. Officers then fired at Matt and they killed the hostage. Is Matt guilty of felony murder?

ANSWER:

108. In anger, Justin assaulted Avi. Avi died from the injuries sustained during the attack. In most jurisdictions, could Justin be convicted of murder using the felony murder rule?

A. No, because the assault would merge with the homicide.

B. No, because Justin could be convicted of murder on other grounds.

C. Yes, because assault is a dangerous felony.

D. Yes, because the felony murder rule eliminates the need to demonstrate malice.

109. One late evening after everyone else had gone home for the night, Ronald and Janie started a fire in order to burn down their office building, so that they could collect insurance proceeds. As they walked down the alley back to Ronald's car, a policeman on patrol stepped out of the shadows and asked them for identification. Ronald and Janie pulled out guns and ran down the alley into the street. Janie wildly fired a shot back toward the alley, thinking that she would stop the policeman. Instead, Janie's bullet killed a pedestrian who was watching the burning building. The police officer ran after Janie and shot her, killing her. Is Ronald guilty of murdering the bystander under the felony murder rule? Of murdering Janie?

ANSWER:

110. What result if Janie and Ronald were charged with murder, but not under the felony murder rule?

ANSWER:

111. The defendant in a felony murder prosecution offered testimony indicating that the prosecution's evidence as to the necessary state of mind for the underlying dangerous felony — armed robbery — might be lacking. As a consequence, the judge gave the following instruction to the jury:

> In order to convict for the crime of felony murder in our jurisdiction, you must find that the government has proven, beyond a reasonable doubt, that the death of the victim here occurred during the commission of the armed robbery of him by the defendant. In addition, you must find that the elements of the crime of armed robbery have been shown by the government, beyond a reasonable doubt.

On appeal, should the court find error?

A. No, the instruction correctly states the jury's obligation in a felony murder prosecution.

B. No, while it did not correctly state the law, any resulting harm was not prejudicial.

C. Yes, the jury is not required to make any finding as to the armed robbery.

D. Yes, the jury is not required to find, beyond a reasonable doubt, the elements of the crime of armed robbery.

112. Hannibal carefully selected his victims. He singled out people whom he felt treated him unfairly or rudely in the past. He claimed to have tortured his victims before killing them. If he is telling the truth, of which crime is Hannibal guilty?

   A. First degree murder, because the killings were premeditated.

   B. First degree murder, because the killings were done with malice.

   C. Second degree murder, because the killings were done with malice.

   D. Voluntary manslaughter, because his victims provoked Hannibal.

113. For more than a year, Lien had been planning to kill Vince. One night, she at last carried out her plan with a single gunshot to the head. Of what homicide crime is Lien guilty?

   A. First degree murder, because the killing was done with premeditation.

   B. First degree murder, because Lien intended to kill Vince.

   C. Second degree murder, because the crime was not gruesome or heinous.

   D. Second degree murder, because Lien intended to kill Vince.

114. The government in a gruesome killing case sought a conviction for first degree murder. It requested that the trial judge give this instruction to the jury as to the necessary state of mind: "An intent to kill, plus premeditation and deliberation, may be formed only moments before the fatal act is committed, provided the accused had some time to think and did intend to kill." Should the judge instruct the jury in this way?

   ANSWER:

115. Spouses Bill and Juanita took a trip to Colorado. Several weeks later, Juanita came back into town without Bill and told her friends that Bill left her on the trip. Juanita was seen around town with several young men after she returned. Neighbors say that Bill and Juanita argued often before the trip. His friends say that he had never suggested that he wanted to leave Juanita. Authorities find that Juanita took out an extremely large life insurance policy on Bill just before leaving for Colorado. Bill has not used his credit cards or accessed his bank accounts since the Colorado trip. Although Bill normally called his son (who lives with his ex-wife) every night and kept in very regular contact with a circle of buddies, neither his friends nor his family have heard from him. Authorities suspect that Juanita killed Bill to collect the insurance money. Can Juanita be convicted of murder even if Bill's body is never found?

   A. Yes, because Juanita had a motive to kill Bill.

   B. Yes, because there is evidence to prove Juanita killed Bill.

   C. No, because there must be a body to prove that a homicide occurred.

   D. No, because there is only circumstantial evidence linking Juanita to the crime.

Manslaughter

116. Pablo and his fiancé Sam got into a huge fight in the mall parking lot. Sam slapped Pablo and called him nasty names. Pablo then seemed to go berserk. He screamed at Sam, took out a pocket knife he carried, and stabbed Sam in the chest. Sam died a few days later from the stabbing. Of what type of homicide is Pablo guilty?

ANSWER:

117. Would your previous answer change if Pablo did not immediately stab Sam? What if Pablo went home, "stewed" about his anger for a few days, then charged to Sam's house and stabbed Sam to death?

ANSWER:

118. Tim's six-year-old daughter Anna had a fever for several days. Although he had been giving her aspirin, her fever continued to rise. One day Anna's fever got to 105 and she began to shake visibly. Tim did not have much money and did not have medical insurance, so he continued to put off taking his daughter to the doctor, out of embarrassment. If Anna died the next day, is Tim guilty of manslaughter?

A. No, because he had no duty to act.

B. No, because he was treating her as well as he knew how.

C. Yes, because he was obligated to get medical attention for Anna and did not.

D. Yes, because his inability to pay for treatment provoked him to act irrationally.

119. Suppose, in the above problem, Tim disregarded advice from his friend, a pediatrician, that he was putting his daughter in serious danger by not bringing her immediately to a doctor. Could he then be convicted of murder instead of involuntary manslaughter?

A. No, the risk is still not great enough.

B. No, a defendant cannot be found guilty of murder unless he intended to kill or cause great bodily harm.

C. Yes, even without the advice Tim would be guilty of murder.

D. Yes, the risk in such a situation is so great and obvious as to allow the charge to be murder.

120. Jerome and Francine had been married for three years. One day at the grocery store, Jerome was picking up some food. A man who he had never met came up to him and said, "Francine and I have been having an affair. She is going to leave you and come live with me." For a few moments, Jerome stood in disbelief. Suddenly Jerome grabbed a frozen turkey from a nearby bin and swung it at the man while screaming, "I'm going to kill you both!" Jerome hit the man on the head several times before running out of the store. The man died soon after from the injuries. Is Jerome guilty of manslaughter?

ANSWER:

121.   Malik started taking a new medication on Friday. The doctor and the pharmacist each warned him not to drive while taking the medicine. The medicine bottle had a prominent label warning against operating machinery, including motor vehicles. Malik noticed that he had been dropping off to sleep all weekend. Nevertheless, he got into his car Monday morning to go to work. There was a construction zone on the highway, so the heavy traffic was moving rather slowly. Malik fell asleep and veered into a car in the next lane. That car swerved and slammed into the concrete construction barricade. Despite the slow speeds, the driver of the other car was killed. Of what crime is Malik guilty?

   A. Murder. Driving in that condition was gross recklessness.

   B. Involuntary manslaughter, because he was criminally reckless.

   C. No crime. He was negligent, but not reckless.

   D. No crime, because the danger was not foreseeable.

KIDNAPPING

122.   Felicia decided to kidnap her boss Eduardo in order to hold him for a ransom. While Eduardo was supervising the clothing section of the large department store where they both worked, Felicia put a knife to his back and demanded that he walk slowly out to the public parking lot across the street from the store. As soon as they got to the parking lot, a police officer observed what was going on, became suspicious, and arrested Felicia. Can Felicia be convicted of the crime of kidnapping?

   A. Yes, once she put the knife to Eduardo's back and demanded that he move, the crime was complete.

   B. Yes, the crime was complete as soon as Eduardo left the place where he wished to remain.

   C. No, Felicia was never able to get Eduardo away from the area by the store.

   D. No, without the use of actual force against the victim, the kidnapping was not complete.

123. What would the result be in the above problem if Felicia did not use force against Eduardo but told him that if he did not go with her, her associate would beat his elderly mother right then?

    A. Same result. Force directed or threatened against any person is sufficient for the crime.

    B. Same result. No force need be shown or threatened for the crime of kidnapping.

    C. Different result. It is only a crime if the force is directed against the person moved.

    D. Different result. A mere threat of force is insufficient for the crime.

124. Suppose, in the problem above, Felicia only kept Eduardo in the parking lot for a minute, then had a change of heart and released him. Would she still be guilty of a kidnapping?

    A. No, that would be too short a time for the victim's confinement.

    B. No, it is only a kidnapping based on a limited confinement if the victim suffers some physical injury.

    C. Yes, any appreciable period of time for the confinement satisfies the element of the crime.

    D. Yes, the crime was complete when Felicia threatened Eduardo.

125. Travis came up to Dr. Rodriguez after his dental appointment was completed at 4:55 p.m. and demanded that she remain in the office suite at 5:00 p.m., after all the staff and patients left. She resisted doing so, at which point Travis told her, "Look, I have a loaded pistol in my backpack. If you don't stay here for another 10 minutes or so, I will shoot you." The doctor remained for 10 minutes while Travis yelled at her about poor quality dental work. At 5:05 p.m., Travis allowed her to leave. Did Travis kidnap the dentist?

ANSWER:

ROBBERY

126. Beth approached a man on a city sidewalk. She showed him a realistic looking toy gun she had concealed beneath her coat and demanded that he give her his travel bag and money. Fearful, the man quickly complied. Has Beth committed robbery?

    A. Yes, because she stole his bag and money.

    B. Yes, the fact that the gun was fake is no defense to the charge of robbery.

    C. No, because Beth was unable to harm him with a gun.

    D. No, because Beth committed no violence against the victim.

127. Pickpocket Patricia encountered Jim on the subway and inconspicuously took Jim's wallet. He did not realize it was missing until much later. Has Patricia committed the crime of robbery?

    ANSWER:

128. Peter approached Nate on the street and told him that he really liked his watch and that Nate should give it to him. Nate refused and attempted to walk away with his son Dante. Peter quickly grabbed Dante, pulled out a pocketknife, and placed it on Dante's neck. Nate immediately relinquished the watch and ran away with Dante. About two hours later, Peter began to feel guilty for what he did, so he spent the rest of the day looking for Nate so he could return the watch. If arrested, could Peter be found guilty of robbery?

    A. Yes, because Peter brandished a weapon when he demanded Nate's watch.

    B. Yes, because Peter originally intended to keep Nate's watch.

    C. No, because Peter did not harm Nate or Dante.

    D. No, because Peter attempted to return the watch.

SEX OFFENSES

129. Emil and Tina were at a party. They did not know each other. Tina was a petite woman, weighing just 105 pounds. Emil was a bodybuilder and weighed well over 200 pounds. Tina drank more than she could handle and went to an upstairs bedroom for a nap. Emil saw Tina go upstairs. Twenty minutes later, he went up and saw that she was asleep in the bed. He pulled down his pants, lifted up Tina's skirt and pulled down her panties. Then, without saying anything, he began to fondle Tina's body, and then laid on top of

her. Tina awoke, looked at Emil, but said and did nothing. She later testified that she did nothing because she was terrified that Emil would harm her if she did. Emil then inserted his penis inside Tina and ejaculated. Is Emil guilty of the crime of rape?

A. No. Emil did not realize that Tina did not wish to have intercourse with him.

B. No. Tina's silence, after opening her eyes, could be taken as consent to the act.

C. Yes. Tina did not consent to the act.

D. Yes. Tina did not expressly consent to the act.

130. Did Emil's action constitute intercourse by force or threat of force?

ANSWER:

131. College student and athlete Paola was studying late in a remote part of the library one night. Coach Bill saw her and sat down next to her and talked with her. He then put his hand on her knee, and she pushed it away. Bill told her that she had to have intercourse with him and that if she refused, he would have her athletic scholarship revoked. Bill then had sexual intercourse with Paola without any voiced objection by Paola. In most jurisdictions, can Bill be convicted of the crime of rape?

A. No, because Bill did not use or threaten physical force.

B. No, because Paola did not expressly object to the sexual act.

C. Yes, because rape is now understood to include coercive acts.

D. Yes, because Paola demonstrated a clear lack of consent.

132. Brandon was 23 years old. Cate was 17 years old. Brandon and Cate met at a college party. Cate's friends are all in college, and Cate routinely used a fake ID to buy alcohol. Given the circumstances, Brandon believed that Cate was 21 years old. Brandon asked Cate out on a few dates. On one of these dates, when Cate's parents were out of town, Cate invited Brandon over to her home and they had sex. The age of consent in this jurisdiction is 18. Is Brandon guilty of rape under the modern approach to rape law?

A. No, because Cate consented.

B. No, because Brandon has a defense of reasonable mistake.

C. Yes, because Cate is under the age of consent.

D. Yes, because Brandon had the necessary state of mind for the crime.

133. Wanda told her husband Harry that she did not want to make love with him anymore. Harry threatened her with a beating, and then over the express objection of Wanda, threw Wanda on their bed and had sexual intercourse with her. Is Harry guilty of the crime of rape?

    A. No. Husbands cannot, as a matter of law, be convicted of raping their wives.

    B. No. Throwing Wanda on the bed is not sufficient to constitute force or threat of force.

    C. Yes. All the elements of the crime are otherwise satisfied.

    D. Yes. The marital status of Harry and Wanda is utterly irrelevant to the prosecution.

134. Can a man be found guilty of raping another man?

ANSWER:

135. Jerald and Gina moved in together about a year after they had started dating. They regularly engaged in sexual intercourse. The police had a valid search warrant and entered Jerald and Gina's home. During the course of the search of the home, the police saw Gina and Jerald having sex in the bedroom. Jerald and Gina are afraid they will be charged with the crime of fornication. Should they be concerned?

    A. No, because fornication laws have been ruled unconstitutional.

    B. No, because fornication laws have been repealed or abandoned in most states.

    C. Yes, because the elements of the crime of fornication were met.

    D. Yes, because the search violated their constitutional rights.

136. After engaging in sexual conduct at one of their homes, two defendants were convicted of violating a state statute which makes it unlawful for two persons of the same gender to have "any contact between any part of the genitals of one person and the mouth of another." Should the conviction be affirmed on appeal?

    A. Yes, so long as the government at trial was able to offer direct evidence of such behavior.

    B. Yes. The state has the power to regulate such behavior.

    C. No. The state does not have the power to regulate such behavior.

    D. No. The statute is too vague and thus violates the Due Process Clause.

Causation

137. Robert and Douglas went riding on Robert's motor boat. Robert said that there was a great area by a rocky outcrop to enjoy water skiing. Douglas, concerned, pointed out the signs near the outcrop which read, "DANGER—Do not swim, boat, or water ski." Robert insisted and drove the boat toward the rocks. After drinking several beers they had onboard, Douglas decided to try waterskiing. Because Douglas had become drunk, he improperly attached the water skis, lost control, and drowned. Is Robert guilty of involuntary manslaughter?

   A. Yes, because Robert insisted on illegally boating in a dangerous location.

   B. Yes, because Robert is responsible for all results of his illegal act.

   C. No, because the cause of Douglas' drowning was his being drunk.

   D. No, because Douglas was contributorily negligent in assessing the risk.

138. Megan invited her friend Trinity to go hiking one weekend. Megan knew that Trinity was terrified of the wilderness. Believing she could help Trinity get over her fear, Megan purposefully became separated from Trinity and left her alone in the wilderness for several hours. Trinity became disoriented and decided to sit against a large tree until Megan could find her. While she was resting, a thick branch from the tree snapped off and landed on Trinity. The blow killed her instantly. Is Megan guilty of involuntary manslaughter?

   A. Yes, because Megan's behavior was negligent.

   B. Yes, because Megan's behavior was reckless.

   C. No, because Trinity dying from a falling tree branch was not foreseeable.

   D. No, because Megan did not intend to kill Trinity.

139. Would the result change if—while alone in the wilderness—Trinity became terrified she would be left there forever, and began breathing heavily, ultimately dying from a heart attack?

   ANSWER:

140. Jessie brutally beat up her enemy Flo. The beating was so bad that Flo was hospitalized and was advised by her doctor that even with surgery, her face would remain horribly disfigured. One hour later, Flo pulled out the feeding tubes that had previously been inserted in her body. The nurses did not discover this until later in the day when Flo was already dead. Is Jessie guilty of a homicide offense?

A. Yes, her action foreseeably resulted in Flo's death.

B. Yes, her action resulted in Flo's death.

C. No, Flo's own action caused her death.

D. No, the negligence of the nurses in not checking Flo more likely caused her death.

141. Eric, ever fearful, hired Jeremy to dig tunnels underneath his house so that he could finish building an underground bunker. Jeremy was free to roam around Eric's basement to do work, but did not have permission to go upstairs to the main area of the house. To support digging his tunnels, Eric provided Jeremy with dozens of faulty extension cords and power strips to supply electricity within the tunnels. While digging one morning, Jeremy notified Eric that there was no electricity or airflow in the basement. Eric, aware that there had been a significant electrical failure recently, waited a few hours to address the problem because he was confident the circuit breaker would reset itself as it had done in the past. Shortly afterwards, Eric noticed smoke coming from the basement and ran outside to call for help. Firefighters struggled to maneuver through Eric's home because of all of his junk, but they were able to put out the fire in a few minutes. Firefighters then found Jeremy's body in the middle of the basement. He died from smoke inhalation. Is Eric guilty of involuntary manslaughter?

A. Yes, because Eric prevented Jeremy from accessing the main floor to escape the fire.

B. Yes, because Eric's actions were reckless.

C. No, because Eric did not start the fire.

D. No, because Jeremy's inability to exit the basement was not foreseeable.

Defenses

SELF-DEFENSE

142. While walking toward the grocery store one evening, Maggie saw a stranger in the parking lot staring at her. Maggie, a petite woman (5'2" and 100 pounds) realized that the stranger was significantly larger (6'5" and 250 pounds). She also noticed that he wore dark clothing and had his coat collar standing up, obscuring much of his face. Maggie completed her shopping and walked back out into the parking lot where she again saw the man, standing about 100 feet from her to her left. She began to walk briskly to her car, parked 100 feet to her right. When she arrived at her car, she looked in the reflection in the car window and noticed the man was moving quickly toward her. While opening the trunk of her car, Maggie could hear the man mumbling incoherently. As she placed the groceries in the trunk she recalled her son's baseball bat was in the trunk. She turned around and the man was now only 10 feet away, still walking toward her. When she saw him reach into his pocket, she grabbed the baseball bat, ran toward him, and swung at him, striking him squarely on the side of his head. Should the court allow a jury instruction on self-defense?

    A. No, because the man did not take any specific aggressive actions toward Maggie.

    B. No, because Maggie was at her car and had a duty to retreat.

    C. Yes, because the man was bigger than Maggie and was acting in a threatening manner.

    D. Yes, because Maggie truly believed that she was in imminent danger.

143. Imagine that the police find that the stranger dropped his car keys in the parking lot and was looking for them when Maggie first arrived and that his apparent incoherence was actually him talking to himself out of frustration at having spent so long looking for his keys. After finding the keys, the man approached his car which was parked next to Maggie's car. Would these facts change the result?

    ANSWER:

144. Assume that Maggie, in the earlier question, chose not to retrieve the bat from the car, but instead threw a cell phone at the man. Would the stranger then be justified if he responded by pulling a gun and shooting Maggie, even if he thought the thrown object was more dangerous than a cell phone?

    A. No, because one cannot use deadly force in self-defense.

    B. No, because the response would not be proportional.

    C. Yes, because a thrown object has the potential to be a deadly weapon, and the creation of such a danger justifies the use of deadly force.

    D. Yes, because the man honestly believed that he was in imminent danger and that the gun was his only means of avoiding injury.

145. Adrianna was on trial for battery. She wanted to raise self-defense to defeat the prosecution case. The trial judge ruled that the defendant would have the burden of establishing, by a preponderance of evidence, the elements as to this defense. Is the judge's ruling correct?

    A. Yes, state law can place the burden on either party as to defenses.

    B. Yes, because self-defense cannot be offered to a non-homicide offense.

    C. No, the government must disprove the defense once the defendant has raised credible evidence as to the elements.

    D. No, the standard of evidence in a criminal case is always proof beyond a reasonable doubt.

146. While watching television at Lenny's house, Lenny and Carl got into a verbal argument. Lenny saw that the argument could escalate quickly and lead to a physical struggle. Lenny stayed stationary. Carl then approached Lenny, gently pushing him against a wall. Would Lenny be justified if he shoved Carl back?

    A. No, because a little shove is not sufficient to make Carl an aggressor.

    B. No, because Lenny has a duty to retreat.

    C. Yes, because Carl was the aggressor and Lenny had no duty to retreat.

    D. Yes, because no one has to accept physical contact without responding in kind.

147. Is the analysis different under modern "stand your ground" statutes?

148. Two uniformed police officers improperly stopped Tien as she walked home. They asked her what she was doing. She brushed past them, remarking that she was going home. The police officers stopped her again, and told Tien that they would like to talk with her. Tien told the officers that she had not done anything wrong, and she attempted to walk away again. The officers then stepped in front of Tien. She fought them, biting, scratching, and pulling the officers' hair. Ultimately, the officers got Tien into handcuffs and into a police car. Was Tien legally justified in her response to the officers?

A. No, because our system protects police officers from being endangered needlessly.

B. No, because Tien started the fight.

C. Yes, because citizens have a right to resist unlawful arrests.

D. Yes, because Tien was outnumbered by the two officers.

149. Would the result in the above problem change if the officers were not in uniform?

150. Sanjay screamed obscenities at Jared. Jared turned and shoved Sanjay. The two exchanged shoves for a short while. Sanjay then pulled a knife and made stabbing motions toward Jared, inflicting Jared with several minor cuts. Can Sanjay claim self-defense for his use of the knife?

A. No, because Sanjay started the argument.

B. No, because Sanjay escalated the altercation.

C. Yes, because Jared started the fight.

D. Yes, because Jared was not hurt badly.

151. Lola and Mel were married eight years ago. After a few years of marriage, Mel began to hit Lola when he would get drunk. Lola tried to move out several times, but Mel always tracked her down and persuaded her to return home. As the years went by, Mel drank more often, and his rages became increasingly violent. Last year, Lola was hospitalized after Mel pushed her down a flight of stairs. A few months ago, Lola was treated for a concussion after Mel hit her with a cast-iron skillet. One day just after that, Mel came home with a gun. He told Lola that the next time she made him mad, he would kill her. Later that night Mel was drinking heavily, and Lola could tell that he was going to be in a violent mood. As Mel walked upstairs, Lola pushed him over the balcony. Mel broke his neck and was killed instantly. Can Lola successfully claim self-defense in response to a murder charge?

A. No, because she should have retreated.

B. No, because she was not in imminent danger.

C. Yes, because, as a battered spouse, Lola knew what was going to happen.

D. Yes, because Mel had been "asking for it."

152. After a late-night shift, Jane walked into a bar to grab a drink. Mike, a long-time nemesis of Jane, found her sitting alone and began to spout derogatory comments about the leather jacket she was wearing. Irate at this insult, Jane walked up to Mike and punched him several times. Seeing this, Barry, the bartender, fetched his baseball bat from the back and swung it at Jane in an attempt to stop the assault. In response, Jane ducked, punched Barry in the face, and ran away. Can Jane claim self-defense for punching Barry under the theory that she was defending herself against the bat swing?

A. Yes, because Jane reasonably believed that Barry posed an imminent threat and that the punch was necessary to respond to the bat swing.

B. Yes, because Jane ran away after hitting Barry.

C. Yes, because Mike started the fight by starting the altercation.

D. No, because Jane is an aggressor who had not withdrawn completely at the time when she punched Barry.

153. Danny and Minho are members of an acting troupe. One late night in the back of a dimly lit parking lot where there were no people around, they decided to practice a fight scene in their latest two-man murder mystery play. It turned out that they were not alone, however, as Janette was sitting in a dark corner taking her break from work at a bar nearby. As Minho, the burlier of the two, raised his fist and engaged in a striking motion against Danny to act out the scene, Janette saw this, sprang to action and beat Minho down to the ground. She believed that Minho was actually attacking Danny. Can Janette be held criminally liable for her attack on Minho?

A. Yes, because Janette did not have a special or contractual relationship with Danny that obligated her to act in defense of him.

B. Yes, because Minho was not actually attacking Danny.

C. No, because Janette was acting under a reasonable belief that Minho was assaulting Danny.

D. No, because Janette had an absolute duty to act to prevent harm to Danny.

DEFENSE OF OTHERS

154. Richard was walking to his car in a busy parking lot. He saw a man step out from behind another car and grab a child. The mother of the child began screaming, "he's got my baby!" The man had no visible weapon. Would Richard be justified in attacking the man?

A. No, because defense of others is limited to those with special relationships.

B. No, because Richard does not have all of the facts.

C. Yes, if Richard uses a reasonable amount of force based on a solid belief that a child was being abducted.

D. Yes, Richard can act because the child would be justified in attacking the man.

155. Assume, in the previous scenario, that the man was actually the child's custodial father, and it was the woman who was trying to abduct the child. Would the outcome change?

A. No, because Richard acted upon a reasonable belief.

B. No, because Richard's actions were not justified under either set of circumstances.

C. Yes, because Richard was wrong in his assessment of the situation.

D. Yes, because the child would not have been justified in attacking his father.

156. Wilfredo walked into a fashionable men's shoe store, tried on a pair of expensive Italian loafers and proceeded to walk out the door wearing the loafers without paying for them. The store employed a plain-clothes security guard, who ran out of the store and tackled Wilfredo on the sidewalk. A pedestrian strolling toward Wilfredo saw the plain-clothes security guard run up behind Wilfredo and tackle him. The pedestrian pried the guard off Wilfredo and punched the resisting guard, knocking him unconscious. Would the pedestrian's actions be justified as a defense of others under the historical approach? Would they be justified under the modern rule?

ANSWER:

DEFENSE OF PROPERTY

157. Melissa left her fancy, expensive car running in front of a store while she went inside to buy some milk. As she walked out of the store, she saw a stranger opening her car door. Melissa yelled and pulled a handgun from her purse. She told the stranger to move away from her vehicle. The stranger looked at Melissa and turned to climb into the car. Melissa shot and killed the would-be thief. In response to a murder charge, can Melissa successfully claim defense of property under the traditional common law principles?

A. No, because shooting someone is never justified.

B. No, because deadly force is not justified solely for the protection of property.

C. Yes, because the use of force is permitted to prevent or stop the imminent theft of property.

D. Yes. Because the car was very expensive, the use of deadly force is warranted.

158. Would the result change for Melissa if she were still in the car and the stranger tried to "carjack" the vehicle?

159. Santiago had just put his two young children to bed and was lying on the sofa reading a novel. He heard a garbage can topple over in his driveway and then heard a window in the kitchen shatter. On his way downstairs to investigate, he took a metal golf club out of his golf bag. Descending the stairs, he came face to face with a burglar standing at the foot of the stairs. Santiago swung the golf club overhead and landed a blow directly to the burglar's skull. Was Santiago justified in acting as he did?

    A. No, because the burglar was not clearly going to injure Santiago.

    B. No, because Santiago should have attempted non-violent methods of preventing the burglary.

    C. Yes, because the use of deadly force is permissible when one's home is invaded.

    D. Yes, because Santiago could reasonably have believed that attempting to stop the burglar with non-deadly force would have put his family in danger.

160. Would Santiago have an easier argument to make if he resides in a state that has adopted a so-called "Stand Your Ground" statute?

DURESS

161. Casey was working at his after-school job delivering pizzas for his family's pizzeria. While waiting at a traffic light, a stranger came to Casey's passenger door, which was unlocked, opened it and sat down in the car. The stranger pointed a gun at Casey and told him to drive him to an address 20 miles away. While Casey drove, the stranger kept nervously checking the rear view mirrors. The stranger instructed Casey to drive faster than the speed limit and to illegally drive on the shoulders of the streets they were on. Casey did so, and also went through several stop signs. After arriving at the destination, the man ran from the car. If brought up on driving charges, could Casey successfully use the defense of duress for the driving offenses?

ANSWER:

162. Suppose the stranger in Casey's car did not flee when they arrived at the destination. Instead, he remained in the car and told Casey they were waiting for his friend. When another man walked out of a building down the street from where they were parked, the stranger said that was his friend. The stranger then repointed the gun at Casey and told Casey to run over the friend with the car. When Casey hesitated, the stranger cocked the gun. Casey put the car into drive, drove up onto the sidewalk and ran over the other man, killing him instantly. Will the defense of duress be successful here?

ANSWER:

163.   Daphne told Raul, her administrative assistant, that she would fire him if he refused to improperly "cook the books." Raul reluctantly did as instructed. When the auditors found the fraudulent entries, may Raul successfully defend against a criminal fraud charge by showing that he acted under duress?

   A. No, because the threat was imminent.

   B. No, because duress may only be used as a defense for threats of deadly force or great bodily injury.

   C. Yes, because Daphne's threat was credible, and she had the ability to carry it out.

   D. Yes, because Raul was not at fault for being put in the threatening situation.

164.   Peter bought cocaine from Mary, who was reputed to be a violent drug dealer regularly threatening her customers into doing illegal things. The day after, Mary went to Peter's house, pointed her gun at him, and told him that she would kill him and his nephews—who lived in a foreign country and could not possibly have been on Mary's radar—if he didn't rob Janet's house. At gunpoint, Peter followed Mary's instructions and took valuables from Janet's house. Can Peter successfully raise the defense of duress at his trial for burglary?

   A. Yes, because Mary's threat to Peter was imminent and immediate.

   B. Yes, because Peter could not have reasonably escaped from Mary's threats.

   C. No, because Peter acted out of concern for his nephews' safety.

   D. No, because Peter acted recklessly by doing business with a known blackmailer.

NECESSITY

165.   Malik was camping in the mountains when a bad storm suddenly hit. Although it was extremely early in the year for a winter storm, several feet of snow accumulated. Malik had no equipment, clothing, or provisions to survive in such severe weather. Slowly clambering through the rocky forest, Malik came upon a cabin. He broke in and for five days he used food and clothing he found in the cabin, until the snow had melted enough

for him to hike back to town. May Malik be excused from the crimes he committed by using the defense of necessity?

A. No, because Malik's lack of preparation caused his predicament.

B. No, because necessity is only available in life-and-death situations, and Malik probably would have survived without committing any crimes.

C. Yes, because the harm Malik avoided (serious injury) was a lesser evil than the harm he created (trespass and theft).

D. Yes, because one may always do whatever is necessary to save one's own life.

166. What result in the above problem if Malik — without any protective equipment or heavy clothing — went camping in the height of winter, and he ignored weather reports speaking of a coming storm?

167. The mortgage company was about to foreclose on Immanuel's house. He knew he had to make a payment immediately, but he did not have the money. Immanuel created a check on his computer with a fake bank account number and sent it to the mortgage company. A week later, Immanuel sent a legitimate check to the mortgage company to make a real payment in order to prevent the foreclosure; he then asked the company to ignore the first check. He was nevertheless prosecuted for a fraud offense. Immanuel raised the defense of necessity, arguing that he was in dire financial straits and had to prevent his home from being taken away, just for a week, until he could make the payment. Would Immanuel's use of the necessity defense be permitted?

A. No, because economic need does not justify the commission of a crime.

B. Yes, although Immanuel could not rely upon the defense under the modern statutes.

C. Yes, because necessity is a defense based on policy, and legislators favor home ownership.

D. Yes, because Immanuel corrected his actions by making the payment as soon as his financial necessity disappeared.

168. Dennis was incarcerated, serving the second year of a five-year sentence. Since Dennis began his incarceration, the conditions at the prison had begun to deteriorate. Pipes dripped waste water into cells, insects and vermin ran rampant throughout the dining areas, and the heating and cooling systems malfunctioned leading to extreme discomfort and illness during winter and summer. Dennis found the conditions to be horren-

dous and he requested a transfer, which was denied. This request angered the guards, who then began to harass Dennis. One morning after a heavy snowfall, Dennis was put on a detail to shovel the walkway leading to the prison yard. Dennis noticed that the plow that had cleared the yard left a large mound of snow next to a fence. When the guard was distracted, Dennis ran up the mound and leaped over the fence. Because the roads around the prison were still being cleared, guards were unable to mobilize quickly enough to chase Dennis. He remained on the loose for almost three weeks before being recaptured. Would Dennis be excused from the crimes related to his escape on the ground of necessity?

A. No, because prisoners should expect poor treatment.

B. No, because Dennis had lawful options available to him.

C. Yes, because any person, including a prisoner, has a right to preserve his own life and health.

D. Yes, because the danger to Dennis' life was imminent.

169. During one winter, a virus outbreak was so intense that most people in the state wore masks in public places regardless of whether they were indoors. That strain of the virus was not particularly lethal for healthier, younger people. Anne, a relatively healthy and young college student, was walking down the narrow hallway of her dorm building while wearing a mask. As she was turning a corner, Anne saw Tom, someone she knew to have caught the virus recently. Seeing that Tom was not wearing a mask, Anne became concerned that she might catch the virus. She immediately turned around, broke into an empty dorm room, and waited for fifteen minutes until Tom passed. On her way out, Anne spotted some masks stacked near the door, so she took one to double up on masks as she left. Would Anne's defense of necessity succeed against the prosecution for her criminal trespass and burglary?

A. Yes, because there was no other thing that Anne could have done to avoid catching the virus.

B. Yes, because not breaking into the dorm room would have resulted in greater harm for Anne.

C. No, because the threat of Anne catching the virus was neither immediate nor imminent.

D. No, because Anne put herself in a situation where there were likely to be unmasked people with the virus.

PREVENTION OF CRIME

170. Mike and Adrianna were the two best sales persons at a local car dealership. As a reward for being named Sales Person of the Year, the dealership awarded one sales person a new car from the lot. The dealership selected Adrianna for this reward. Mike believed he should have received the award and became incensed when it was given to Adrianna. Deciding to claim what he believed was rightfully his, Mike went to Adrianna's home. Finding nobody home, Mike peered through the garage window and saw Adrianna's new car inside. Unable to open the garage door, he pried open the garage window and was half-way through when police officers out on a routine patrol saw him and yelled for him to halt. Mike climbed back out of the window and then began to walk toward the backyard of Adrianna's house. The police twice told him to stop moving. When Mike began to run, one officer fired her gun at Mike, striking him with two bullets in the back. Does the officer have a defense of "crime prevention" (or "law enforcement") in response to a criminal charge?

    A. No, because police officers may not use deadly force in effectuating an arrest.

    B. No, because Mike was fleeing but appeared unarmed.

    C. Yes, because Mike just committed a felony.

    D. Yes, because the officer knew that Mike would get away if she did not use force to stop him.

171. Would the result for Mike change if he had a pistol in his hand and screamed at the officer, "Leave me alone or you'll be sorry"?

172. Gus, an undercover police officer, was having coffee in a diner at around 6 a.m. He was sitting at the counter when he heard a man and a woman, who were seated in a booth behind him, discussing how they had paid for their previous night's revelry by holding up two convenience stores. He heard the woman announce she needed to use the bathroom in the back, and then heard the man say that the woman should see if the diner's cash register was as helpful as the other registers they had encountered. Even though he had finished his coffee and needed to leave, Gus decided to see if the couple was serious or if he had misunderstood them. He saw the woman come from using the bathroom and approach the register. The woman then put her hand in her coat pocket as she began speaking to the diner's cashier. Gus, thinking the woman was about to pull a gun, rushed from his seat and tackled the woman. May Gus use the defense of crime prevention against a charge of battery?

    A. No, the force used was too extreme.

    B. No, because force may only be used to make an arrest after the completion of a crime, not to prevent a crime.

    C. Yes, because Gus had reason to fear for his safety.

    D. Yes, because use of force is permissible to prevent crimes.

173. One night, Ollie broke into an unoccupied house. He used a short five-inch metallic screwdriver to unlock the door, picked up some jewelry lying around, and headed back out into the street, the screwdriver and his hands in his pocket. As Ollie was exiting the house, Officer Buddy discovered Ollie about fifteen feet away. Knowing the house to be unoccupied and seeing that the door was pried open, the officer told Ollie to stop where he was standing. Ollie turned around with his hands still in his pocket, took out his short screwdriver, and began running towards the officer. Seeing the lights reflected on the screwdriver, Officer Buddy thought Ollie was holding a small handgun in his hand and fired his gun at Ollie without warning. Ollie sustained severe injuries. Would the court find that the officer's use of deadly force was justified?

    A. No, because Officer Buddy did not warn Ollie that he would use deadly force if Ollie did not comply.

    B. No, because what Ollie was actually holding was a non-lethal screwdriver, not a handgun.

    C. Yes, because Officer Buddy had probable cause to believe that Ollie posed a serious physical harm.

    D. Yes, because Officer Buddy was trying to apprehend Ollie.

ENTRAPMENT

174. Known drug dealer Leon asked Cynthia if she was interested in making "some good money" because he could "hook her up with some fine stuff." Cynthia told Leon that she just got out of prison a month before for a drug offense, and she did not want to get mixed up with that kind of business again. A few months later, Leon heard that Cynthia desperately needed money. He again asked Cynthia if she would like to make some money. When Cynthia hesitated, Leon described how easy it would be, how much money she would make, and how safe it would be. Leon assured Cynthia that he had clients with whom he could connect her so that she need not risk getting caught in an undercover drug bust. Finally, after several more meetings and much coaxing, Cynthia said that she would help sell the drugs, but only until she got back on her feet. Leon was actually an undercover drug agent who had Cynthia arrested when she tried to make her first sale from the drugs Leon had provided. Under the majority subjective test would Cynthia have a successful defense of entrapment?

    A. Yes, because the government supplied the drugs.

    B. No, because Cynthia willingly committed the crime.

C. No, because Leon's actions were not overly coercive.

D. Yes, because Cynthia was not predisposed to commit the crime when Leon first contacted her.

175. What result if Cynthia, above, was not at all reluctant but immediately agreed to sell the drugs?

176. Assuming the same facts here, but under the objective test (used by some states and adopted in the Model Penal Code), would Cynthia have a successful defense of entrapment?

A. No, because Cynthia willingly agreed to deal drugs.

B. No, because Cynthia was predisposed to deal drugs.

C. Yes, because Leon's persistent actions induced Cynthia into criminal activity.

D. Yes, because Cynthia gave up drug dealing earlier.

177. Alice had four prior convictions for prostitution, the most recent being five years ago. Late one night, as she was walking down the street on her way home from a club, a car pulled up next to her. The man offered her twice what she used to make for a sexual act. Alice adamantly declined. As she continued walking down the street, the man drove alongside her and doubled his offer, making it four times the amount customers normally paid for such acts. Alice hesitated, but decided that she could not afford to pass up so much money and agreed to perform the illegal act. The man turned out to be an undercover police officer and had her arrested. Does Alice have a successful defense of entrapment, using the subjective test?

A. No, because Alice was predisposed to engage in prostitution.

B. No, because Alice performed the illegal act for the money.

C. Yes, because the police officer offered an irresistible amount of money.

D. Yes, because Alice appears to have given up prostitution years before, and seemed reluctant at the start.

178. A sting operation was created to catch high school students suspected of selling illegal drugs to middle school students. Fernando was a high school student who had been arrested for selling drugs. In exchange for Fernando's assistance, the prosecutor agreed to drop the pending drug charges against him. Acting as an undercover agent, Fernando asked students who had sold drugs for him in the past to sell drugs again. They readily agreed, and Fernando gave them drugs provided to him by the police. Once arrested for

selling the drugs, the students claimed that they were entrapped. Will their defense be successful under the subjective test of entrapment?

A. No, because the students were already drug dealers and were not reluctant to continue selling drugs.

B. No, because Fernando was not a police officer.

C. Yes, because they were selling drugs provided by the police.

D. Yes, because they would not have agreed to sell the drugs if they had known that Fernando was working for the police.

179. Two tests are used in the United States to determine whether a defendant has been entrapped. The majority subjective test is based on the "predisposition" of the defendant to commit the crime. The objective test considers the behavior of a reasonable person in response to the actions of the government. A number of states (California, Michigan, Iowa, Texas, et al.) have adopted the objective test. Which of the following considerations forms the primary basis for the objective test?

A. People who are culpable should be held accountable.

B. The judicial branch should provide a check against the executive branch.

C. Looking to the culpability of the individual defendant, courts can evaluate whether that person would have committed a crime without government inducement.

D. The police need a wide range of options in the efforts to reduce crime.

180. For a long time, marijuana had been grown unlawfully in Wayne's field. Earlier this year, Wayne was convicted of marijuana possession. Wayne harvested the field twice in the last five years, selling the hemp for clothing production. He also had other brushes with the law. Three years ago, Wayne was convicted of selling marijuana. Recently, law enforcement officials made a deal with Dustin, a drug dealer, to buy a large quantity of marijuana from Wayne. Dustin placed the order and paid for the shipment with money provided by the government. After selling the marijuana to Dustin, Wayne was arrested. He claimed that he was entrapped. Under the majority view, which pieces of evidence may the government introduce to show that Wayne was not entrapped?

A. Wayne had marijuana growing in his field.

B. Wayne was previously convicted of possession of marijuana.

C. Wayne was previously convicted of selling marijuana.

D. All of the above.

181. Thanh served several years in prison for murder after being hired to build and plant a car bomb. A few months after her release, an undercover police officer approached Thanh, explaining that he knew of her bomb-making ability and complimenting her on her abilities. He then asked if she would consider building and planting another bomb for a potential client. After several rounds of negotiation, Thanh agreed to the project. She constructed the device and attached it to the car of the victim, a drug dealer the district attorney had been unable to successfully prosecute. Thanh sat with the under-cover police officer in his car, waiting for the target to enter his sabotaged vehicle. When he did, Thanh activated the remote detonator, which exploded the car and seriously wounded the drug dealer. As soon as this took place, the undercover police officer arrested Thanh. Under either of the two tests, was she entrapped?

   A. No, because a defense of entrapment is not available for attempted murder.

   B. No, because Thanh did not complete the crime that the officer had paid her to do.

   C. Yes, because the police exceeded the bounds of propriety in hiring her to kill a person.

   D. Yes, because she would never have committed murder without the officer's inducement.

182. Duane's drug lab was shut down after the police arrested his chemist on other charges. Noah, an undercover officer, agreed to help Duane get the illegal lab running again. Soon, they were actively producing large quantities of drugs. Once the business was running and Noah was involved in it, Duane recruited Farah to help with packaging and distribution. Both Duane and Farah were later arrested for manufacturing and dis-tributing drugs. Both argued that they were entrapped. Assuming that Duane is ac-quitted of the charges after the jury accepted his defense of entrapment resulting from police over-involvement, should the jury also find that Farah was entrapped?

   A. No, because Duane was not a government agent.

   B. No, because Farah was willing to participate.

   C. Yes, because all third parties are accorded the entrapment defense if the primary defendant is successful in raising the issue.

   D. Yes, because the entire business would not have existed, but for the government's participation.

183. Louis was a smuggler. He claimed that he could get anything into the country from Asia. An undercover officer asked Louis to smuggle rare antiques. Louis knew it was illegal to import such items. Louis agreed and delivered the antiques. Was Louis entrapped according to the majority test?

   ANSWER:

184. Under the facts in the previous question, was Louis entrapped according to the minority test?

ANSWER:

INTOXICATION

185. Reese attended a college football game with some old college buddies. Even though his friends knew he often drank to excess, they permitted him to drink alcohol. Reese was intoxicated before the game and continued to drink during the game. Reese's school was defeated in the football game, and he and his friends retreated to a bar to continue drinking. A fan of the rival team was in the bar and jokingly teased Reese and his friends about the game. Reese became angry at the man and shoved him off of his barstool. The man stood up and attempted to walk away, but Reese continued shoving him. As Reese persisted in shoving the man, they moved in the direction of a large mirror hanging on the bar's wall. Eventually, Reese pushed the man into the mirror and caused it to shatter. A shard of glass penetrated the man's neck and he bled to death. The next day, Reese remembered going to the bar but did not remember anything after that. Under the majority rule, can Reese claim his intoxication as a defense to murder?

A. No, because a defendant's intoxication can never be introduced as evidence for the defense.

B. No, because there is no complete defense of intoxication.

C. Yes, because Reese is an alcoholic, and it is unconstitutional to punish someone for such a disease.

D. Yes, because Reese's intoxication prevented him from having the capacity to form the intent to murder.

186. In the previous problem, on what grounds could evidence of voluntary intoxication allow Reese to escape all criminal liability for the killing?

ANSWER:

187. In a prosecution in which the defendant is charged with attempted murder, the defendant offered evidence of extreme intoxication at the time of the crime. What would be an appropriate instruction to the jury in most jurisdictions?

    A. If you find that the defendant killed the victim, but was too inebriated to be fairly held for her actions, you must find her not guilty.

    B. If you find that the defendant killed the victim, you may not consider any evidence of her intoxicated condition because intoxication is not a defense.

    C. If you find based upon the totality of the evidence that the government did not demonstrate that the defendant intended to kill, then you must find the defendant not guilty.

    D. You must find that the defendant intended to kill in order to return a guilty verdict. You may not consider, on this issue, her level of intoxication.

188. Brandi was invited to a party at the home of her friend Luis. When she arrived, Luis encouraged her to drink some punch. Brandi declined, telling him that she was "trying to cut down on the liquor I drink." In response, Luis said, "No problem, there's no alcohol in the punch." Brandi then drank several large glasses of the punch. Unbeknownst to both Brandi and Luis, another guest had secretly "spiked" the punch by putting in a large amount of a potent drug. The drug caused Brandi to go berserk, yell at Luis and then slug him in the face with a large wooden bowl. Luis died soon thereafter from the blow to the head. Brandi is charged with murder. Can she claim involuntary intoxication as a defense?

    A. Yes, because her intoxication was truly involuntary. As she did not intend to take any drug, she could not have foreseen the effects.

    B. No, it is common knowledge that all sorts of ingredients go into punch. For this reason, Brandi accepted that risk when she drank the punch, so her intoxication was not involuntary.

    C. No, because involuntary intoxication is not a defense to a violent criminal charge.

    D. No, because Brandi voluntarily became intoxicated when she drank large amounts of the punch.

189. Would the result above change if—before drinking the punch—another guest had said this to Brandi: "I wouldn't drink that stuff, I hear it's been spiked with something weird."

ANSWER:

THE INSANITY DEFENSE

190. At his trial for first degree murder in the killing of his girlfriend, Fernando claimed that he heard voices from God at the time directing Fernando to kill his girlfriend to prevent the world from coming to an end. While he did not want to kill her and knew that it would be illegal, Fernando believed the voices in his head and thought that Armageddon would result if he did not kill her. Fernando raised the insanity defense. The defense expert testified that Fernando attempted to get psychiatric help in the past for his condition, but that all of the doctors had failed in their treatment. This doctor further testified that Fernando's condition could be remedied by a regimen of anti-psychotic drugs. In fact, by the time of the trial, such a program had already succeeded in restoring Fernando to a nearly normal condition. Since Fernando had been seeing this particular doctor, he no longer suffered from the extreme hallucinations and uncontrollably violent rampages that destroyed his professional and personal life up until the time he killed his girlfriend. Which of the following would be the most appropriate jury instruction in a majority of jurisdictions?

A. If the killing was the product of a mental disease, you must find the defendant not guilty.

B. If the defendant did not know the difference between right and wrong at the time of the killing and if the killing was a result of mental impairment, you must find the defendant not guilty.

C. If the defendant could not control his impulse to kill even though he was aware it was wrong, you must find the defendant not guilty.

D. If the defendant, as a result of a mental disease or defect, lacked the substantial capacity to appreciate the wrongfulness of his conduct or to conform his conduct to the law, you must find the defendant not guilty.

191. Assume that Fernando's case is tried in a jurisdiction that adheres to the *M'Naughten* test of insanity. Can the judge exclude evidence that Fernando heard voices instructing him to kill?

ANSWER:

192. Would it be appropriate if the judge also excluded testimony from a defense expert that "Fernando suffered from a mental illness which caused him to kill his girlfriend"?

A. Yes, because experts are not allowed to testify to the ultimate issue of insanity.

B. Yes, because such evidence is irrelevant to a case under the *M'Naughten* rule.

C. No, because the jury is entitled to hear all evidence which pertains to a defendant's mental capacity at the time of the killing in order to make an informed decision.

D. No, because a qualified expert is allowed to present his professional opinion to the jury.

193. The state legislature has, for more than a century, followed the traditional *M'Naughten* standard for insanity in criminal cases: "The party accused was laboring under such a defect of reason, from disease of the mind, as not to know the nature and quality of the act he was doing; or, if he did know it, that he did not know what he was doing was wrong." In an attempt to limit the reach of the insanity defense, the law makers changed the standard so that only the second portion of *M'Naughten* is now used in the state. Defendants, therefore, can only prevail on the insanity defense if they can show that as a result of mental illness, at the time of the alleged crimes, they "did not know the criminal act was wrong." Is this new standard constitutional?

A. Yes, no constitutional issue is raised by the change.

B. Yes, the legislature has the power to alter the traditional test, even if the new standard is considerably more narrow.

C. No, narrowing the standard would violate the due process rights of criminal defendants.

D. No, because the *M'Naughten* test was developed by the courts, the legislature does not have the power to change the test.

194. TRUE OR FALSE. In a majority of states, the burden of proof as to the insanity defense is on the defendant. Explain.

ANSWER:

195. Assume that Dabney has decided not to present an insanity defense at trial. He and his attorney concluded that the government will likely not be able to prove all the elements of the murder charge. Moreover, even if the government were to win the case, Dabney does not want to be sent to a mental institution, a consequence of a successful insanity defense in his state. At trial, the defense introduced some evidence about Dabney's unstable and confused mental state for the past several years, hoping the jury would conclude that Dabney could not have formed the necessary intent to kill. One of Dabney's friends described several instances in which she found Dabney sitting in a room alone, responding to voices that he seemed to be hearing. This testimony concerned the trial judge who believed that Dabney was severely disturbed and deserved to get psychiatric treatment in a hospital, not a lifetime in the prison system. The judge raised the insanity defense over Dabney's objections, and instructed the jury accordingly. Was this action erroneous?

A. No, because it is in the judge's discretion to raise the defense if it seems that Dabney could be found insane.

B. No, the judge is obligated to raise the defense if it seems that Dabney could be found insane.

C. Yes, the judge's action deprived the defendant of the ability to strategize about his defense with his attorney.

D. Yes, because it is very unlikely that a jury would find Dabney not guilty based on the insanity defense.

DIMINISHED CAPACITY

196. Abigail was arrested and charged with the first degree murder of a child for whom she formerly babysat during the daytime. When questioned, Abigail stated that she could not remember anything about the day the murder supposedly occurred. At trial, the defense presented psychologists and family members. They testified that Abigail was suffering from severe emotional problems at the time the child was killed. The behaviors Abigail exhibited at that time were indicative of someone suffering from mental illness. However, the defense did not offer the insanity defense. This led the prosecution to assert that all the testimony regarding Abigail's mental state was improper. Should the defendant have been allowed to offer such evidence?

A. No, at least with respect to the family members, who were unqualified to speak to this question.

B. No, because such testimony is irrelevant if Abigail is not offering the insanity defense.

C. Yes, because all the evidence might relate to the state of mind requirement and is therefore relevant in disproving the murder charge.

D. Yes, because the jury could find the defendant insane even if the insanity defense has not been raised.

197. In the previous case, what would be an appropriate instruction on this evidence?

198. Dory has a history of serious mental illness. She has been charged with assault after a bizarre encounter with a neighbor. Her lawyer does not wish to raise the insanity defense, but does want to offer evidence of her mental illness to show that she did not have the necessary intent to commit the charged offense. Citing established state law, the trial judge ruled that she could only offer such evidence if Dory raises the insanity offense. Dory's lawyer contends that the trial judge's ruling is improper as it violates due process principles. Is she correct?

   A. Yes, the defendant has a due process right to raise all evidence which the trier of fact might find helpful in resolving a material issue in the prosecution.

   B. Yes. If the judge's ruling were proper, all sorts of evidence could be restricted that could violate the due process rights of defendants.

   C. No, judges always have the discretion to limit evidence that can be offered by either side in a criminal case.

   D. No. Because of special concerns about evidence regarding mental disease, the state may give the judge wider discretion to limit evidence that might be confusing to the trier of fact.

COMPETENCY TO STAND TRIAL

199. After being arrested for felony murder, Sarah awaited trial in jail. She began to display signs of severe mental disorder. She carried on conversations with non-existent persons, attempted to inflict wounds on herself when police questioned her, and insisted that she was sent back in time from the future to save civilization from destruction. Should Sarah's lawyer raise this matter pre-trial?

   A. No, this information would be relevant at trial in disproving the ability to form the state of mind required for the crime.

   B. No, this information would be helpful at trial in offering a defense to the crime.

   C. Yes, the lawyer should raise the matter before trial in connection with an insanity defense.

   D. Yes, the lawyer should raise the issue of competency to stand trial in light of this evidence.

200. TRUE OR FALSE. The competency determination looks to the time of the trial, not the time of the crime, to determine the defendant's mental state.

Practice Final Exam

201. Carolina became very drunk while out with her boyfriend Fritz and other friends. The couple had been having difficulties for some time and often argued. Very late that evening, Carolina got a ride home from one of their mutual friends, Andrew. An hour later, Fritz appeared at her apartment, claiming that she had been unfaithful to him when she left the pool hall with Andrew. Fritz then slapped Carolina. She responded by yelling, "I hate you and never want to see you again." She slapped Fritz hard and then pushed him, causing him to fall down the stairs to the basement. Fritz died after hitting his head on the steps. If the government demonstrates that Carolina intended to kill Fritz, of what crime will she most likely be convicted?

    A. First degree murder.

    B. Voluntary manslaughter.

    C. Negligent homicide.

    D. Nothing, because she could successfully raise the defense of intoxication.

202. Javier hated his next-door neighbor because of what Javier thought was the ugly and over-the-top sort of house the neighbor built. Javier was going to destroy that horrible residence. His plan was to go over to the neighbor's house when the family was out of town, set fire to the house, and watch it burn down. He did go over to the neighbor's house when the family was out of town, and tried repeatedly to set a fire with a detonating device that he had invented. He was unsuccessful at setting a fire or even an explosion, but a passing police officer saw Javier trying to set a fire and arrested Javier. Is Javier guilty of arson?

ANSWER:

203. What crime is Javier guilty of?

204. Ken was on a long road trip and decided to pick up a hitchhiker named Danny on the side of the highway. The stranger looked a little odd, but seemed nice and the two traveled for an hour or so together. Ken then said he needed to get some gas. Danny told Ken he planned to "hit up the place" so he could get some cash. Danny showed Ken his loaded pistol and jokingly said that Ken could consider the free gas his contribution for the ride. Ken said nothing about the proposed crime but pulled into the nearest station. After Ken gassed up his car, and while Danny was in the store, Ken jumped in his car and drove off to the highway. He never reported anything to the authorities about Danny. After robbing the station, Danny was apprehended and told the police of his conversation with Ken. Can Ken be found guilty of conspiracy to commit armed robbery?

A. No, because he never agreed to commit the crime and he may have been acting under duress.

B. No, because Ken withdrew from the plan, providing him an affirmative defense.

C. Yes, because Ken helped Danny by bringing him to the right place, by following his instructions, and by not reporting the crime immediately.

D. Yes, because an agreement to rob the store can be inferred from the actions of the pair.

205.   What if Ken and Danny actually knew each other previously? If they were cellmates in a county jail some time before serving sentences for similar convictions for theft and armed robbery, would the result change?

ANSWER:

206.   Warrenetta and Matt concocted a plan to kidnap a college student named Tamara and not release her until her parents paid them $1 million. The two agreed that no weapons were to be used at any time and that Tamara was not to be harmed in any way. Matt was supposed to wait by Tamara's college dormitory and lure her to a van by asking for her help carrying some packages. Tamara was suspicious, but Matt managed to get her in the van. As they were driving out of the city to a mountain cabin to hide out, a tractor-trailer slammed into them. The accident was not Matt's fault, but Tamara died several days later of her injuries. Can Matt be convicted of murder?

A. Yes, because he intended to kidnap her and did so, he can be found guilty of felony murder.

B. Yes, because he intended for her to die.

C. No, because he did not intend for her to die.

D. No, because he did not intend for her to be hurt and the accident was unforeseeable.

207. Suppose, in the previous problem, that Tamara did not get into the van willingly. Matt then pulled out a weapon and threatened her. They struggled and the gun went off, killing Tamara. Warrenetta, who was waiting in the driver's seat, had no idea that Matt had a gun. Can Warrenetta, nonetheless, be convicted of murder?

    A. Yes, because she would be responsible for Tamara's death, even if the death was unforeseeable.

    B. Yes, because she was a co-conspirator in the kidnapping and therefore can be found responsible for the foreseeable actions of her co-conspirator and the consequences of that conspiracy.

    C. No, because the killing was accidental.

    D. No, because unlike Matt, Warrenetta had nothing to do with Tamara's death. They had agreed that no weapons of any kind would be used.

208. Funnyman Dai decided to, in his words, "scare the daylights out of that pompous Kevin." At a party, Dai told everyone what he was going to do once Kevin got there. When Kevin arrived, Dai pulled out an obviously fake pistol and pointed it at Kevin. All the other partygoers started laughing and one of them yelled, "Oh Dai, stop being so funny and put away that toy." Kevin was not amused. He punched Dai in the face. After being charged with battery, will Kevin be able to establish a successful self-defense claim?

ANSWER:

209. Alice was found guilty of conspiring to commit armed robbery. She and several acquaintances had planned to rob a local bank. According to the testimony of the arresting officers and the other co-conspirators, Alice exhibited signs of mental illness. She often had conversations with imaginary people, she sometimes dressed in combat gear in preparation for "the coming alien invasion," and she had a history of treatment in mental health facilities. A few key rulings from the trial are being questioned at the appellate level. Defense counsel never raised the insanity defense at trial. Nonetheless, at one point during the defense presentation, the defense lawyers elicited the testimony of Dr. Wee, a renowned mental health expert. At the conclusion of the trial, the judge provided an instruction as to the insanity defense even though counsel objected to the instruction. Was the evidence of mental illness relevant if defense counsel did not put forth the insanity defense at trial?

    A. No. The mental condition of the defendant should not have any bearing on the outcome unless the insanity defense is presented.

B. No. The mental illness of the defendant is not relevant in a conspiracy case.

C. Yes. Counsel may have been arguing that the government failed to prove its case beyond a reasonable doubt.

D. Yes. The evidence clearly demonstrated that the defendant did not know right from wrong.

210. In the previous question, was the trial judge's instruction proper?

A. No, because his instruction violated Alice's right to decide the manner in which defenses were raised at trial.

B. No, because Alice could be mentally ill and therefore incompetent to stand trial.

C. Yes, because an insanity instruction could only help the defendant.

D. Yes, the judge has the ultimate duty to ensure that the defendant receives a fair trial.

211. Suppose in the same case that the defense did raise the insanity defense. The defense attorney asked two questions of its expert witness. First, "Doctor Wee, does the defendant suffer from a mental illness?" Second, "On the day in question, could she, as a result of her mental illness, understand the difference between right and wrong?" Over the objection of the prosecution, the judge allowed the witness to answer both questions. To the first question, he stated, "Yes, I think she does have a mental illness." To the second, he said, "It is difficult for me to say with any certainty, but I believe that she probably did not understand the difference between right and wrong." Should these questions and answers have been allowed?

ANSWER:

212. Walt owned a general store next to a high school. From the hours of 2:00 p.m. to 4:00 p.m., he usually sold a large quantity of potent household cleaners, mostly to kids stopping by on their way home from school. At times, it seemed odd to him that he sold so many of these kinds of products, considering the nature of his store and the fact that his teenage son never helped out with the housework. He asked his son about this and the boy said that lots of teens were into "huffing" cleaning solvents. Wanting to preserve the profits of the store in any way he could, Walt expanded the selection and the number of cleaning products he sold. A teenager who routinely bought cleaning products from Walt was found dead as a result of inhaling the fumes from a cleaning solvent. The evidence showed that the product that caused the teen's death was purchased two days earlier from Walt's store. Could Walt be found guilty of a homicide offense?

ANSWER:

213. Betty is a private nurse who worked and lived in Martin's household. Betty was the only member of the household staff who saw widower Martin on a regular basis. Martin's doctor advised complete bed rest and quiet, and warned that with his deadly heart condition any other lifestyle would hasten his death. Betty grew to dislike Martin intensely. One day, Betty was in the house when Martin hit the "panic button" beside his bed. This button was only to be used when he needed emergency medical attention. Hearing the buzzer, Betty remembered she had not given Martin his heart medicine that morning. Nevertheless, she decided to finish folding the linens before she went to look in on him. An hour later, when she checked on him, Betty found Martin dead. Can Betty be found guilty of a homicide offense?

    A. Yes, because she committed actions that led to his death. By failing to give the medication and then delaying her response to the "panic button," she engaged in grossly reckless behavior.

    B. Yes, but the only conviction could be on a charge of negligent homicide.

    C. No, because in most states the criminal law does not impose a duty to act to help someone in need.

    D. No, because Betty did not cause Martin's death.

214. Dirk and Eric were opposed to the federal government's foreign policies. The Secretary of State came to their town to give a speech to community leaders, and Dirk and Eric decided to join in a protest demonstration. They arrived at the meeting hall and linked up with several groups opposing the administration's foreign policy. When the group of government cars, including the Secretary of State's, arrived at the meeting hall, Dirk and Eric threw rice at the cars and yelled, "Send Food Not Bombs!" When the Secretary was walking into the building, they used very powerful bullhorns and screamed at her, calling her a murderer and a criminal. Dirk and Eric were quickly arrested for violating a state law that provides the following: "A person is guilty of disorderly conduct when in a public place, and with intent to cause public inconvenience, annoyance or alarm, he or she makes loud, disturbing and unnecessary noise." What challenges will Dirk and Eric raise at their trial for violating the law?

ANSWER:

215. At 11:00 p.m. an anonymous tip was received by the village police department that a burglary was about to occur at a particular jewelry store. The dispatcher notified all patrolling officers. Officer Briscoe was just a few blocks away and made it to the location within a few minutes. Officer Briscoe did not witness any suspicious activity at the store, but he noticed the entrance to the store also permitted access to an apartment above the store. A second officer, Officer Lopez arrived, and the two of them rang the doorbell of the apartment. No one answered. At the same time, the officers heard a clatter coming from the apartment's fire escape around the corner. As the two officers rounded the corner to investigate, they saw a man dressed in black holding a satchel leap from the fire escape onto the sidewalk. Officer Briscoe yelled for him to stop. The man turned to see the police officers, and then ran off in the opposite direction. Officer Lopez went back to his car while Officer Briscoe began to pursue the man on foot. Officer Briscoe knew he could not catch the man, so he yelled "stop or I will shoot you!" The man kept running, so Officer Briscoe took aim and fired two shots, striking the man in the neck. The suspect died en route to the hospital. Although no weapons were found on him, the satchel he was carrying contained several jewels that the owner of the store identified as belonging to her. If Officer Briscoe is charged with killing the unarmed suspect will he be able to successfully assert a defense?

A. No, because the fleeing felon doctrine only applies if the suspect was attempting to commit, or fleeing from, a felony.

B. No. Because the suspect did not pose a serious and immediate danger to the officer or to others, Officer Briscoe had no justification for shooting him.

C. Yes, under the fleeing felon doctrine, if the officer had a reasonable belief that the suspect was a fleeing felon, then the actions can be justified.

D. No, under the fleeing felon doctrine, the officer is not justified in killing a suspect, only in wounding him to prevent further flight.

216. Bertha and Adam were college sweethearts. They were crushed to learn that Bertha was pregnant. They delayed making a decision as to the baby. When the time arrived, Adam delivered the child at a secluded farmhouse, using knowledge he learned from researching on the web about childbirth. Immediately after the delivery, Adam handed the child to Bertha. She looked at the child, looked at Adam and said, "we can't keep this child." Adam took the child, brought it to the barn and suffocated it with a towel. Medical testimony at the murder trial of Adam will indicate that the child lived for less than five minutes. Will this testimony defeat the murder prosecution?

A. Yes. It was not clear whether the child would have survived even with proper attention.

B. Yes. Adam was under no duty to assist the child.

C. No. Even five minutes of life is sufficient to show that a homicide took place.

D. No. Adam would have been guilty even if the child had not survived the birth process.

217. Alicia raised the entrapment defense at her trial for a white-collar offense. The judge, over the objection of defense counsel, gave this instruction to the jury:

The entrapment defense can only be effective if the defendant has shown that she was not predisposed to commit the offense at the time she took a step toward the commission of that crime.

Is this a correct statement of the law?

A. Yes, the burden of proof can be placed on the defendant with this defense.

B. Yes, the focus of the defense is the moment just before the crime is committed.

C. No, the focus of the defense is at the moment when the government first seeks to have the defendant commit the crime.

D. No, it is improper to place the burden of proof on the defendant with this defense.

218. Jeremy is on trial for the crime of rape. He claims that he had sexual intercourse with the victim, but that it was consensual. His lawyer advised him against accepting a plea bargain offered by the government because, the lawyer said, Jeremy has a very strong case. This view is based on the defense team's investigations, which turned up a witness who can testify that, a year previous, he had sex with the victim. In addition, the victim's "open" lifestyle might lead the jury to conclude that the encounter was consensual. Is the advice of Jeremy's attorney sound?

A. Yes, because lack of consent is not an element of a sexual assault charge.

B. Yes, because the previous sexual encounter would be strong evidence for the defendant.

C. No, because even if the defense lawyer demonstrates that the victim had previously had consensual sex with others, it does not prove that she had consensual sex on the occasion in question.

D. No, because the defense attorney will likely be barred from offering this evidence.

219. Juana hated her local grocery store. The long lines, poor customer service, and high prices made her angry. She regularly complained to the store manager, on several occasions claiming that she wanted to burn the place down with all of the employees and customers inside. On a particularly busy day at the store, Juana became extremely frustrated at the crowds and inattentive service. She saw the manager in one of the aisles and yelled at him, exclaiming, "This is terrible! I am burning this place down as soon as I finish my shopping! You should have listened to me!" The manager shook his head and told his colleague that he could not wait for the day Juana moved away. A few minutes later, that colleague noted Juana was at the cashier and was purchasing several cans of instant lighter fluid, the type someone might use to ignite a barbecue grill. Remembering her threat to burn the store down, he informed the manager and called the police.

Juana was arrested in the parking lot as she carried her bags to her car. Based only on these facts, can Juana be convicted of attempted murder?

A. Yes, because her intent to kill is certain.

B. Yes, she took a number of steps on the road to a murder.

C. No, her steps were merely acts of preparation.

D. No, it would not be attempted murder until she began to set fire to the crowded store.

220. Would the result change in the above problem if—at midnight when the store closed—the manager saw Juana standing right outside the store carrying a large bag?

Answers

Limits on the Criminal Sanction

1. **The correct answer is C.** The Supreme Court held, in *Robinson v. California*, 370 U.S. 660 (1962), that it would violate the Constitution for the government to criminalize a disease or status such as narcotics addiction. Under a more traditional analysis, **answer A would be incorrect** because it is not at all clear that the officer's observation alone would be sufficient evidence upon which to convict with the standard of proof beyond a reasonable doubt. The standard is whether reasonable jurors could find sufficient evidence to conclude, beyond a reasonable doubt, that the government has proved each element of the crime. *Victor v. Nebraska*, 511 U.S. 1 (1994). While the officer's observations, taken with Dawn's statements, could well be enough to convict, **answer B is incorrect** because the statute would be found to be invalid on constitutional grounds, as noted above. **Answer D is wrong, too.** Apart from other problems with the prosecution, Dawn's statements could otherwise be admissible against her. Under the facts here, the statement would not involve serious questions under either the Fourth Amendment (unreasonable searches and seizures) or the Fifth Amendment (privilege against self-incrimination). Because Dawn's statements would fall within a recognized exception to the hearsay rule for admissions, it also would not raise a question under the rules of evidence.

2. **Yes.** While Dawn could not be convicted of a crime directly related to her disease or status, as indicated above, the rule is quite different regarding affirmative acts committed, even acts committed in furtherance of one's status. Thus, if Dawn was charged with burglary, and she could show that she stole in order to support her need for illegal narcotics, the trial court would reject such evidence concerning the reason for the burglary. The Supreme Court in *Robinson* held that the actions of an addicted person are subject to criminal sanctions, even though the status of that same person would not be similarly subject. Appearing in public while under the influence falls within the scope of actions taken. A conviction might be allowed because the punishment would not be merely for an addict's status.

3. **The best answer is A.** As noted in Answer 1 above, the Supreme Court held that an addict could be punished for committing crimes in furtherance of her habit, *Robinson*. However, in *Powell v. Texas*, 392 U.S. 514 (1968), a majority of the Court found that punishing someone for being drunk in public would violate the Constitution if the person could show that she had nowhere else to go. If Dawn could demonstrate her addiction and her lack of private space in which to take drugs, the conviction would fail.

Answer B is not the best answer because it fails to address the issue of whether Dawn's presence in public is based upon her voluntary choice to leave her home while under the influence. In this case, because Dawn had nowhere else to go, she may successfully argue that her arrest amounted to an impermissible prosecution based on her status as an addict that would not occur with persons who had other alternatives. Thus, **answer D is wrong. Answer C is not correct.** While **answer C** presents another possible constitutional bar to criminal statutes, it is not operative here. Citizens must be given fair notice of laws which prohibit behavior. Publication constitutes fair notice. Because the statute in question gave proper notice here, Dawn could not successfully argue that she lacked knowledge of the illegality of her conduct.

4. **No.** Just as in the above questions, the Eighth Amendment prohibits criminal punishments for individuals who are acting involuntarily—such as due to addiction or homelessness. Since sitting and sleeping on the sidewalks are unavoidable consequences to being involuntarily houseless, the city cannot pass a law that would criminalize that involuntary behavior. *See Jones v. City of Los Angeles*, 444 F.3d 1118 (9th Cir. 2006).

5. **Answer B is correct.** The officers can arrest Alexander for violating the ordinance because there is shelter available for Alexander to go to, allowing him to comply with the ordinance. Because shelter is available, Alexander's camping in the park is voluntary, and the facts of this question do not criminalize involuntarily houselessness; therefore, **answer C is incorrect.** Since there is another option, Alexander's action would be considered voluntary, and therefore, he is in violation of the ordinance just as any person found camping in the park would be. While the officers may arrest Alexander for violating the ordinance, they cannot arrest him for being houseless, as his status is not a crime, and he is protected from being punished for his status under the Eighth Amendment; **answer D is incorrect. Answer A is incorrect** because the officers cannot force Alexander to go to a shelter, regardless of their stated motivation.

6. **Yes.** The Constitution requires that a statute be reasonably clear and certain, so that the average person could understand its meaning. Otherwise, a court may declare the law void for vagueness and invalid under the Due Process Clause. *Kolender v. Lawson*, 461 U.S. 352 (1983). This result stems from the guarantee of due process, which prohibits punishing a person for violating a law that is generally unintelligible. Because judges recognize the difficulty legislators face in crafting criminal codes that adequately anticipate future conduct, the courts are reluctant to strictly invoke this doctrine. For this reason, even laws that an experienced lawyer might have a difficult time comprehending are often upheld despite vagueness challenges. Still, the term "unsafe driving" is not at all definite and there is no historical meaning attached to it. *Tanner v. City of Virginia Beach*, 674 S.E.2d 848 (Va. 2009). Thus, the challenge to the statute will likely succeed.

7. **Yes.** Even absent a statutory definition for the phrase "reckless driving," if courts in the jurisdiction (or even other jurisdictions) have interpreted its meaning, or if the phrase

has roots in common law jurisprudence, the statute will likely survive a vagueness challenge. Here, the phrase "reckless driving" has been invoked, applied, and interpreted repeatedly to include conduct such as Bashira's. Likewise, an argument that the average person would not know that Bashira's behavior was reckless would be unsuccessful. The challenge to the statute will likely fail.

Elements of the Offense

THE ACT

Failure to Act

8. **The correct answer is D.** Generally, the criminal law imposes no duty to act to help others. This general rule remains true even in situations in which a failure to act seems morally reprehensible. The law is clear in refusing to impose an obligation to act. *People v. Erb*, 894 N.Y.S.2d 266 (N.Y. App. 2010). Hence, **answers A and B are incorrect.** Because the "no duty" rule usually applies even to those with great skills or expertise, **answer C is incorrect.**

9. **Yes,** Zion would now likely be found guilty of a serious homicide offense. While individuals normally do not owe any duty of assistance to strangers, such a duty exists in limited situations, such as those involving close familial relationships (*see* question 11). Zion agreed, as part of his employment situation, to assist accident victims either by providing aid or advising others to do so. A contractual relationship, if breached, can also give rise to a criminal standard of care. By not fulfilling his obligation, he has caused great harm and will be found criminally responsible. *Commonwealth v. Pestinikas*, 617 A.2d 1339 (Pa. 1992).

10. **The best answer is B,** as most states have hit-and-run statutes which require those involved in a serious accident, even those who are not at fault in causing the accident, to either render assistance or report the incident. Alaska Stat. § 28.35.060; Cal. Veh. Code § 20003. Thus, **answer D is incorrect.** While Troy is obliged to act here, it is because of a statutory duty, not a moral duty, so **answer A is wrong. Answer C is incorrect** because the statutory mandate concerning those involved in serious accidents is an explicit exception to the generally accepted rule of no duty to others.

11. **The correct answer is A.** When the victims of crimes are children, many jurisdictions impose special responsibilities to act on their behalf. *Staples v. Commonwealth*, 454 S.W.3d 803 (Ky. 2014). Without question in this case, Matthew owes his children that special responsibility as he is their father and was in a unique position to discover and prevent the crime of abuse. **Answer B is incorrect** as Matthew, the young girl's father, would be responsible for the abuse even if he did not pose a specific question

to his daughter. Because Matthew is her father, he is expected to be involved in her life and take actions to ensure that she is safe. For this reason, **answer C is also incorrect. Answer D is certainly true** insofar as Matthew's ex-wife is primarily responsible for the abuse. However, this does not answer the question as to Matthew's culpability which exists apart from his ex-wife's liability.

12. **Maybe.** While generally there will not be such reporting obligations, some states have — by statute — imposed such a duty on those who work closely with children, such as teachers. 23 Pa. C.S.A. § 6311; Code of Virginia § 63.2-1509.

13. **No,** for Marianna had not taken any steps in furtherance of her plan. The law punishes culpable intent together with actions, but the criminal law does not punish mere thoughts. *People v. Landof-Gonzalez*, 163 N.E.3d 15 (N.Y. Ct. App. 2020) (dissenting opinion). The criminal law's act requirement stems partly from practical reasons; we cannot be sure of another person's thoughts if no action has been taken upon them. Moreover, the act requirement recognizes that people may think horrible thoughts, including wishes to seriously harm others, but that many of these people will never act upon their thoughts. In this case, even if Marianna fully intended to carry out her plan, she might not have gone through with it. Therefore, no criminal charge can be maintained against her.

The Voluntary Act

14. **The best answer is A.** The law can only punish those who act consciously and voluntarily. *State v. Hinkle*, 489 S.E.2d 257 (W. Va. 1996). Because the cause of the accident was the unknown brain disorder, Betty will not be found guilty of any crime. **Answer C, then, is wrong.** While offering to drive her friends was a conscious and voluntary act, the specific cause of the accident was her disorder, not her offer, so **answer D is also wrong. Answer B does not apply to this situation.** Once the offer of the ride was made, Betty would be responsible generally for her friends, though not here where she was unaware of her medical problem.

15. **Yes,** Betty could now be held responsible. The chargeable criminal act here would not be unconsciously going off the road. Rather, it would be getting into the car with her friends and knowing of the substantial risk that her medical condition could result in serious dangers to all of them. Under those circumstances, her knowledge, coupled with her behavior, would make for clear culpability and criminal liability. *State v. Miser*, 208 P.3d 808 (Kan. 2009).

16. **The instruction is error.** It is the prosecution's obligation to prove — beyond a reasonable doubt — all elements of the charged crime. Consciousness is part of the requirement for a voluntary act, thus the burden cannot be shifted to the defendant to disprove the element. *Mullaney v. Wilbur*, 421 U.S. 684 (1975).

17. **The best answer is C.** Courts generally imply a requirement of voluntary action even if the statute or ordinance in question does not specify such a requirement. Judges will imply such an element because of the importance of the *actus reus* requirement throughout the history of the common law. Such a mandate is thus viewed as intended by the legislature, even if not explicitly included. Here, it seems likely that a court would see Binh's drunkenness as a voluntary action, but not his decision to go into public while drunk. If the officers' conduct appears to be intended to lure him into public space in order to arrest him for the crime, the defense will have a winning voluntariness argument. *State v. Eaton*, 177 P.3d 157 (Wash. App. 2008). Since the courts usually imply a voluntary act requirement, **answer A is incorrect.**

Answer B is not correct, even though courts usually have little tolerance for excuses made for drunkenness, as shown in the later problems involving intoxication as a defense. Here, however, it does not appear that Binh intended to venture out in public, and that he did so only under coercion by the police. A factfinder would certainly have enough evidence to conclude that Binh's walk to the sidewalk was involuntary, and that the act requirement implied in the statute was absent. Even though the elements of the crime might otherwise be shown, Binh could not be convicted. For this reason, **answer D is also incorrect.**

18. **Yes.** Although Elise, of course, did not intend to harm anyone, she had proper notice that her medication may cause issues and she was warned by both her doctor and the medication label not to operate machinery while taking the medication. Though her lightheadedness was involuntary and caused her to release the crane, she voluntarily chose not to take the appropriate action called for by her medication label.

19. **Yes,** Elise can be held criminally responsible. While neuroscientific research is still being explored regarding consciousness and awareness, the law recognizes a difference between being asleep and falling asleep. In *State v. Olsen*, 160 P.2d 427 (Utah 1945), for example, the defendant fell asleep while driving and unintentionally ran over a pedestrian. The Utah Supreme Court found that the defendant was responsible for allowing himself to be in a condition where he could fall asleep and cause an accident without his awareness.

Here, Elise voluntarily showed up to work in the middle of the night and fell asleep due to her tired condition. While the ultimate result of her decision to come to work and operate the crane was involuntary, her choice to put herself in a position where she could fall asleep and cause such harm was not.

THE MENTAL STATE

20. **The correct answer is C.** The required state of mind for the statute is knowledge. This is interpreted to mean that an actor can be held responsible for injuries to his child, under the statute, if he was subjectively aware that his child was at risk. *Fabritz v. Traurig*, 583 F.2d 697 (4th Cir. 1978). The prior similar episode, along with Tamika's known violent temper, would likely be enough to find Rick guilty of the crime. In cases such as this, Rick would be held culpable because, among other reasons, his knowledge of the situation put him in the best position to prevent the harm to his children. **Answers A and D are wrong** because Rick did have the opportunity to realize the threat to his children. If, however, there were no prior incidents to create this knowledge on Rick's part, and Tamika did not have an especially violent temper, **answer B would be correct.**

21. **Yes.** Without the earlier incident it would be very difficult for the government to prove beyond a reasonable doubt that Rick had "knowingly" subjected a child to significant injury or neglect.

22. **The correct answer is D.** Drunken driving in many states is considered a strict liability crime. These crimes require no showing of a particular mental state. *Staples v. United States*, 511 U.S. 600 (1994). Strict liability crimes are highly unusual in the criminal law because the question of culpable mental state is central to our society's determinations of appropriate criminal sanctions. Other than answer D, each of the other responses contends that Ellie did not have the requisite state of mind to be convicted of driving while intoxicated. Many such criminal statutes have no state of mind requirement, beyond knowledge of driving after consuming alcohol. Although most criminal laws have a specified or implied *mens rea* requirement, no additional state of mind is required for a conviction in this case. The mere act of drinking and driving has been determined to be of such significance that the act alone can permit culpability. Thus, **answers A, B, and C are incorrect** because none of the claims would further Ellie's defense that the act alone can permit culpability.

23. **The best answer is B.** Many jurisdictions have created the crime of reckless endangerment to punish actions such as those in this case, in which the recklessness of an actor caused serious injury, but for which homicide charges are unavailable because the victim survived. **Answer A is not the best answer** because attempted murder would not likely be a successful charge against Ellie. Although her actions threatened the child's life, she did not act with intent to harm the child. Attempt crimes always require that the defendant act purposefully or with intent, as explained below. **Answer C is not correct.** The charge of manslaughter would be a viable option, and Ellie's most likely conviction, had the victim died. Because the child lived, this charge is unavailable to the prosecutor in this case. The fact that manslaughter varies from the crime of murder only in terms of the state of mind needed does not affect this requirement. In all homicide cases (including manslaughter), the victim must have died. *State v. Kramer*, 2021 WL 4123422 (N.M. 2021). Because the child survived, manslaughter could not be charged. For the same reason, **answer D is not correct.**

24. **The correct answer is A.** The intent to injure here can be found under the doctrine of transferred intent. *Cruz v. State*, 2021 WL 5176655 (Nev. 2021). The most common explanation for this theory is that the necessary intent "follows" the action. If the defend-

ant intended to punch someone, although he actually hit another person, he remains culpable in terms of the resulting injury. **Answer B is incorrect** because the statute explicitly requires proof of intent. No societal purpose would be served if answers C or D were true. **If answer C were correct**, the defendant would only be held responsible for his intentional acts if he had better skills at throwing punches. Similarly, **if answer D were true**, a defendant could be exonerated merely because the intended victim had been rude to the man who punched the actual victim.

25. **The correct answer is C.** In proving the mental state of knowledge, the key issue is whether the defendant herself knew the true nature of her activity. The issue is not whether a reasonable person would have known the activity was criminal (an objective standard) because knowledge requires a subjective determination. Therefore, **answer B is incorrect. Answer A is also incorrect**, as the government has conceded that Kayla did not know of the criminal activities. **Answer D is wrong** because the statute requires a showing of knowledge.

26. **The correct answer is C.** Most jurisdictions require that the defendant must have been personally aware of the risk involved in order to be convicted of criminal recklessness. *Brasse v. State*, 392 S.W.3d 239 (Tx. Crim. App. 2012). This subjective requirement is much more stringent than the usual tort negligence standard, which speaks of only a substantial deviation from the standard of care. Therefore, **answer B is not the best answer.** Answer A refers to that standard of negligence, which allows the finder of fact to conclude that a defendant should have been aware of the substantial, unjustifiable risk, and finds him responsible for his acts or omissions. Recklessness, as noted above, means a personal, subjective awareness of the risk. Because this criminal statute adopts a standard higher than negligence, **answer A is wrong. Answer D is also incorrect.** If Randy's behavior is found to be reckless, he will likely be determined to have caused the child's injury despite the troop leader's inattentiveness.

27. **No.** If Victoria did not mean to inflict harm upon her boyfriend, she will not likely be convicted of intentional wounding. The state of mind of intent requires that a defendant purposefully cause the harm prohibited by the crime. *People v. Felix*, 92 Cal. Rptr. 3d 239 (Cal. App. 2009). Regarding the facts of this case, Victoria does not appear to have acted with intent to cause harm with the knife. While the struggle might have been reckless due to the presence of the large knife, the requirement here involves far more than subjective awareness of a substantial risk. Unless the government can show a true purposeful act to harm the boyfriend, the prosecution will fail.

28. **Maybe.** Under these facts, a judge or jury might find that dropping the knife was intentional, not accidental.

29. **Answer D is incorrect** in that the mistake presented here is one of fact, not one of law. Trisha believed she was entering her own apartment; she is not asserting that

she believed breaking into her neighbor's apartment was legal. Often the distinctions between mistake of law and mistake of fact are less than clear, but not here. **Answer A is incorrect** in that mistake of fact does not provide an affirmative defense. An affirmative defense supposes that the accused is guilty of the crime, but for policy considerations — such as the conclusion that people should be able to provide a reasonable level of self-defense — the defendant can be exonerated. No such defense exists merely because the defendant was mistaken. **Answer C is also incorrect** because burglary requires an intent to enter someone else's dwelling. **Answer B provides the best response.** While Trisha cannot offer this evidence as a true defense, she will likely be able to present evidence as to her mistake in order to negate the government's contention that she intended to break in and steal from her neighbor's apartment. Such an approach is an assertion that the government has failed to establish a required element of the crime, the element of intent. *United States v. Smith-Balither*, 424 F.3d 913 (9th Cir. 2005).

30. **Maybe.** A showing of intent is required for the attempted murder charge, so the mere act of planting an explosive device that appeared dangerous on a train would not be enough to convict. The government must demonstrate beyond a reasonable doubt that it was Ivan's purpose to kill or seriously injure others. If Ivan is believed, he could avoid such a conviction as he knew that the bomb could not explode. The argument that a killing would be impossible under the circumstances will provide no defense. The question relates to the Ivan's knowledge, his intent. If he is believed as to his state of mind, he will prevail on this charge. If, however, he is not believed, the factfinder could conclude that the defendant intentionally took all steps necessary to carry out his plan, and the defendant will be convicted of attempted murder.

31. **Yes.** The charge of reckless endangerment involves subjective awareness of a substantial risk. If the government could show the defendant knowingly planted a bomb — even an inoperative bomb — on the train, that element would be satisfied because placing a bomb in such circumstances was a reckless action that could lead to harm or injury as it did here.

32. **The best answer is C,** as courts typically do not allow the advice of private counsel to be used in defending against a criminal charge. Any other approach would put lawyers in an uncomfortable position because their clients could benefit from bad legal advice. *United States v. Impastato*, 543 F. Supp. 2d 569 (E.D. La. 2008). **Answer A is wrong,** for although his reliance could have been reasonable, Jorge may still have had the necessary *mens rea* to be found guilty of the crime. For that reason, **answer B is not the correct answer.** Finally, because few crimes are strict liability (as noted earlier), the statute here would most likely require at least knowledge of his actions. Thus, **answer D is also wrong.**

33. **Yes.** The result changes dramatically if Jorge has relied on a statement of the law given to him by an individual charged with construing or enforcing the law. Because a citizen could properly assume that the head of the Office on Environmental Control has the authority to give advice on a matter relating to pollution, Jorge's reliance would be viewed as reasonable. It could, then, be offered as a defense of mistake of law. The courts allow this defense under these circumstances, as to do otherwise would enable the government to prosecute citizens who properly and timely seek government approval of their actions. In a sense, the defense is truly an estoppel principle.

Parties to Crimes

34. Under the common law, parties to a crime, those not as directly involved as the perpetrators of the crimes themselves, were criminally responsible based upon the premise that all culpable individuals should be punished. *Standefer v. United States*, 447 U.S. 10 (1980). For this reason, **answer A is not the correct response.** Under the common law, Tabitha can be held liable as a party to the crime, even though she was not directly involved in the criminal enterprise. A principal in the first degree must have committed at least one element of the crime in question and must have been present at the scene of the crime. Because keeping watch for the authorities is not an element of the crime of armed robbery, Tabitha would not be a principal in the first degree under common law rules, so **answer B is incorrect. The best answer is answer C** because Tabitha truly was a principal in the second degree. Under the common law, a principal in the second degree must have provided some assistance in the commission of the crime and must have been present at the scene of the crime. Although Tabitha could argue that she was not actually at the scene of the crime (that she was only having coffee next door), such an argument would likely prove unsuccessful as she was in the immediate vicinity. If, however, Tabitha was able to successfully argue that her presence at a cafe next door to the bank was not sufficient to make her present at the scene of the crime, **answer D would be correct.** Under the common law, a party would be considered an accessory before the fact if she provided some measure of assistance toward the commission of the crime, but was not at the scene of the crime. It is important to remember that the above-described common law distinctions have fallen out of favor, and relatively few jurisdictions maintain meaningful distinctions based on this rubric. Instead, the modern approach of a majority of jurisdictions in determining the liability of parties focuses on the defendant's state of mind and the level of assistance offered, as indicated below.

35. Under the modern approach regarding parties to crimes, a determination as to whether individuals other than the perpetrators are participants in crimes is judged by an involvement and intent standard. Tabitha's liability will be determined both by her activities and by her purpose to participate. *People v. Moomey*, 123 Cal. Rptr. 3d 749 (Cal. App. 2011). After considering these elements, a trier of fact will be able to determine whether Tabitha can be held liable as an accessory after the fact, defined as a person who renders aid, comfort, and/or shelter to the criminal (even though she was not present during the commission of the crime). Although Tabitha's involvement in helping to hide the criminals would be sufficient to find her culpable as an accessory after the fact, her intent in relation to her actions must also be resolved. If Tabitha thought that her boyfriend was joking about robbing a bank, one could conclude that she did not have the requisite intent, as judged by both objective and subjective standards, to participate in any part of the crime. If, however, Tabitha knew that her boyfriend had robbed banks in the past and, for this reason, Tabitha truly understood that he was not joking about the reason he wanted to go to the cabin, Tabitha could be found to have the sufficient intent to be held responsible for assisting in the robbery after the fact.

36. **The best answer is answer D.** Under the modern approach, a person can be held liable as a party to a crime if the person's involvement in the crime and her intent to participate in the crime are shown. *Huntley v. State*, 769 S.E.2d 757 (Ga. App. 2015). Here, however, the manager was unaware that Sophie intended to harm the employee when he provided Sophie with the employee's name. Merely providing information to Sophie without the intent that a crime occur is not sufficient to establish liability for a party to a crime. **Answer B is not the best answer** because Sophie did not make her intentions clear until *after* the manager had told her the employee's name. **Answer C is wrong** because if the manager had known Sophie's intentions when the manager gave the employee's name, then the manager might be held responsible as a party to the crime. **Answer A is not correct** because the manager did not know Sophie's intentions when he gave Sophie the employee's name. As discussed above, in order to be held liable, the manager would have had to be aware of Sophie's intentions when he gave Sophie the name.

37. **Yes,** the result would change if the manager gave Sophie the employee's name after the manager became aware of Sophie's intentions. Virtually any action can be considered sufficient to establish guilt as a party to the crime if a person knew of the principal actor's intentions and purposefully took actions in order to further those intentions. Here, after learning of the intention of the principal actor Sophie, the manager gave the name of the employee, which helped Sophie in her endeavor.

38. A person can be held liable as a party to the unplanned crime of another that occurs during the commission of a planned crime if that other crime could have been foreseen as a predictable occurrence associated with the planned crime. Wis. Stat. § 939.05. **The correct answer is answer A.** Aisha did not intend for an assault to occur, only a burglary. Because the assault of a person in the house was not a natural and foreseeable consequence of the burglary Aisha intended, she will not be held responsible for the assault, even though she may be held responsible as an accomplice to the burglary. Although Aisha committed an act in furtherance of the assault (driving Jason to the house), she did not know of or intend for the assault to occur, nor should she have foreseen the assault. For this reason, **answer B is incorrect. Answer D is also incorrect.** Aisha will not be held culpable as a party to the crime of assault because Jason did not act within the scope of the contemplated crime and because his actions were not foreseeable by Aisha (but not because she did not know that such actions would occur). **Answer C is an incomplete answer** because it fails to examine which crime Aisha intended to commit together with her partner Jason.

39. Yes, Aisha can be considered responsible as an accomplice to the owner's murder. Unlike the assault described above, the possibility of a violent altercation with the homeowner in the process of burglarizing a home is a foreseeable consequence of the burglary. The fact-finder can determine that Aisha has accepted the consequences of the burglary to the extent that they were foreseeable. On this basis, the trier of fact could hold Aisha liable as an accomplice to the owner's murder because she could have reasonably anticipated such an event when her partner entered the house.

40. The best answer is answer D. Although Amanda could be seen to have encouraged Lance in his action, that view is only available in hindsight. Words alone will rarely demonstrate both the action and intent necessary to find one culpable as a party to a crime unless it can be shown that the person in question had some knowledge or belief that her words would encourage someone to commit a particular crime. Here, it is unlikely the government could show that Amanda meant for her comments to lead to violence. Although Lance was encouraged in his actions by the remarks Amanda made, that encouragement may not be enough to render Amanda guilty as a party to Lance's crime. Furthermore, there is no indication that Amanda intended for harm to come to Lance's boss, although she might have felt that the woman "deserved" it. Therefore, **answer A is incorrect.** Similarly, **answer B is not the best answer.** Because Amanda's remarks were not sufficient to create criminal liability in these circumstances, a clear showing of intent is also needed. *McMillan v. State*, 850 S.E.2d 779 (Ga. App. 2020). **Answer C** points to the possible constitutional argument against allowing a person's words to be held against her. However, the First Amendment's protection of speech is not absolute and this answer fails to address the nuances of such an argument. Under the Constitution, a person is entitled to criticize laws and to advocate the violation of criminal laws in an abstract sense. However, the First Amendment does not protect those who incite others to break the law by encouraging the commission of specific crimes. *United States v. Schulz*, 529 F. Supp. 2d 341 (N.D.N.Y. 2007). Although it is unlikely that Amanda could be found liable for her remarks, her lack of criminal liability results from the fact that her speech did not evince the requisite intent or incitement, not from any constitutional protections associated with her speech.

41. The best answer is answer C. Many jurisdictions provide for the opportunity of a party to abandon or withdraw from a criminal endeavor. However, Al did not meet those requirements. In order to effectively withdraw, Al would have had to voluntarily and completely relinquish his purpose and make a substantial effort to prevent the crime from taking place. *United States v. Duncan*, 578 Fed. App'x 183 (4th Cir. 2014). This would have required Al to tell the others of his intent to quit the project or to try to stop them in their purpose, probably by contacting the police. Because Al did not take either of these actions, he did not legally withdraw from the kidnapping. As such, Al would likely incur liability as a party to the crime of kidnapping. For the same reason, **answer A is incorrect. Answer B is incorrect** because Al did involve himself in the crime. In order to initially incur responsibility, the endeavor must have involved some preparation.

Here, Al participated in extensive preparation for the crime. **Answer D is also incorrect** because many jurisdictions do provide an opportunity to withdraw.

42. Unlike Al, who will clearly not be considered to have properly abandoned the enterprise, the issue of Chen's abandonment is more complicated. Chen did attempt to end the endeavor by trying to dissuade Jenkins from continuing in the plot. Chen also contacted the police, which satisfied one requirement of abandonment. Nevertheless, he could probably not escape liability for two reasons. First, the kidnapping was complete with the taking of the child, so there was no pending crime from which to withdraw. Second, even if withdrawal was possible, whether his withdrawal from the enterprise was *voluntary* remains unclear. Generally, one is not considered to have *voluntarily* withdrawn from a crime unless one is motivated by a change of heart. *State v. Simon*, 2021 WL 3508414 (Oh. App. 2021). This signifies, at least, that one should not by motivated by fear of failure in one's criminal goals or by a mere concern that arrest is imminent. To the extent that Chen is able to convince a factfinder that his altruistic sentiments were the motivating factors in his decision to abandon the plot, Chen may be able to argue that he withdrew effectively. Such an outcome is unlikely.

43. **The correct answer is A.** Even though Stefano no longer wanted to be involved, he did not make his intent known because of his worry about upsetting Angelica. A change in intent is not enough to terminate his role in the commission of the crime, so **C is incorrect. D is incorrect** because Stefano did not withdraw from the crime. In order to withdraw, Stefano would have had to make his disapproval known to Angelica sufficiently in advance of the break-in to give her the chance to reconsider her involvement, as well. *See State v. Formella*, 960 A.2d 722 (N.H. 2008). Without an affirmative action to convey his disapproval, Stefano participated in the theft as an accomplice and did not withdraw his involvement. **B is incorrect** because it does not address the possible withdrawal defense.

44. **Not in most jurisdictions.** Gerald will lose the argument on appeal. As most courts consistently have noted, there is no "dependency between aiding or abetting and the offense that is aided or abetted." Most courts allow the conviction of one defendant for bribery to stand — in one trial — even though the other person was found not guilty of receiving the bribe — in another trial. So long as the jury in such a case finds, beyond a reasonable doubt, both that the defendant gave a bribe and that it was received, it is appropriate to hold the defendant criminally responsible. The mere fact that another jury reached a different result in another prosecution is irrelevant. Such a situation "does no more than manifest the simple, if discomforting, reality that 'different juries may reach different results under any criminal statute. That is one of the consequences we accept under our jury system.' While symmetry of results may be intellectually satisfying, it is not required." *Standefer v. United States*, 447 U.S. 10 (1980).

The Inchoate Offenses

SOLICITATION

45. To find Kiara guilty of solicitation, the government must prove that she intended that the crime be committed and took some act in furtherance of the crime, usually in the form of active encouragement or inducement. *United States v. Southern*, 2021 WL 3884294 (S.D. W. Va. 2021). While such intent is usually proven by circumstantial evidence, if the only evidence against her is a casual remark at a social gathering, Kiara is unlikely to be found guilty of solicitation. If, however, she was found to have intended that Peter murder his wife, and therefore found guilty of solicitation, her subsequent comment to Peter that she was not seriously suggesting he get rid of his wife will likely not defeat the solicitation charge. In many states, one cannot successfully withdrawal from a solicitation once sufficient encouragement has occurred. As soon as the suggestion or request has been made, the crime is complete, so a later change of heart will not bar her conviction for solicitation even if the intended crime never occurs.

46. **D is the best answer.** While each of the items might not be enough to persuade the trier of fact of Kiara's intent, taken together the messages — communicated in different formats — might well be persuasive in showing a true purpose of Kiara to have Peter harm his wife.

47. **The best answer is D.** The act requirement for solicitation is that a person request or encourage another to commit a crime. The crime also contains a mental state requirement — intent that the crime be committed. The difference between casual conversation and true solicitation to commit a crime is often one of degree, and therefore a conviction for solicitation may fail for a lack of intent even if a sufficient act might be shown. On these facts, it appears unlikely that the government could prove that Steven truly intended that Miguel commit this crime. However, with more concrete evidence of intent, Steven could indeed be found guilty of solicitation. Therefore, **answer B is incorrect.** For example, had Steven said to Miguel, "You ought to give that guy what he deserves and slash his tires," the government might be able to prove he had the requisite state of mind. **In such a case, answer B would be correct. Answer A is wrong** because it does not appear that Steven suggested that Miguel carry out the crime. **Answer C is incorrect** because solicitation does not require a significant or affirmative act toward the crime by the solicitor, only a statement or action manifesting encouragement or support for another committing that crime.

48. **The correct answer is A.** Regardless of whether or not the person solicited to commit the crime would accept the request or encouragement, if the elements are otherwise shown, the crime of solicitation has taken place. *People v. Gordon*, 120 Cal. Rptr. 840 (Cal. App. 1975). The reason for the criminalization of solicitation is to punish the culpable intent of the solicitor, so the ability or desire of another to act on the solicitation is irrelevant. Here, Hanh demonstrated the requisite intent to acquire drugs and requested that another person provide them, allowing her to be found guilty of solicitation. **Answer C is therefore incorrect. Answer B is wrong** because the officer's status is irrelevant; the proof element goes to Hanh's state of mind. A payment of money could establish true intent for the solicitation, so **answer D is also incorrect.**

49. **The best answer is D.** Solicitation can take place without effectively communicating the request or encouraging the intended person. As Tony believed he was soliciting the crime, he can be seen as just as culpable as if he had communicated the request to have Pete assaulted. Therefore, **answer C does not provide the best explanation.** It is possible Tony could argue that he never intended to communicate the request because he knew the letter would not be mailed. **Answers A and B are wrong**, as they deny Tony's culpability in requesting Pete be injured, while both the intent and act requirements of solicitation appear to be met here.

50. **The best answer is C.** The man's comment (after the other, earlier acts) that he was trying to sell "stuff" (not "pies"), adds convincing circumstantial evidence that he intended to solicit purchasers of illegal drugs. While a jury or a judge could find the circumstantial evidence convincing enough to convict, the man's comment makes the case much more clearly one of solicitation. His comment helps establish the intent behind his actions. Thus, **answer D is not the best answer. Answer A is incorrect** because circumstantial evidence alone can establish guilt for any crime. *State v. Davis*, 155 A.3d 221 (Conn. 2017). Usually, the difficulty in obtaining convictions lies in establishing intent through circumstantial evidence. In this case, the man's statement to the officers effectively resolves any doubt concerning his state of mind (i.e., he was in fact not a baker attempting to sell pies). Therefore, **answer B is also incorrect.**

51. To successfully charge Brigid with solicitation, the government must prove that she intended the crime against Adam to be committed and that she took some act in furtherance of the crime, such as encouraging Camille to "teach Adam a lesson." *See State v. Owens*, 480 P.3d 184, at *3 (Kan. App. 2018). Even though both Camille and Brigid were intoxicated, Brigid still intended for Camille to "put Adam in his place." Voluntary intoxication does not serve as a defense to solicitation. Therefore, both **answers C and E are incorrect. Answer D is incorrect** because, while Brigid did not specifically tell Camille to crash his car, she did discuss various ways for Camille to "put Adam in his place," including encouraging Camille to damage his car and taking the action of identifying Adam's car for her. Because it is Brigid's intent that matters here—not Camille's—**answer B is also incorrect. The correct answer is A.**

ATTEMPT

52. **The best answer is B.** The attempt offense requires both the intent to commit the crime and, in most jurisdictions, some sort of substantial act in furtherance of the crime. Although Sally's intent to murder her husband and Katia may be clear from her enrollment in the auto class and her confessed plan, Sally had not yet tried to implement this plan. Action toward the crime is required for attempt because the law does not penalize bad thoughts alone. It could be argued that enrolling in the auto class was sufficient action towards implementation of the crime, but this is unlikely to be found a substantial enough step for criminal liability. Sally still had many more acts remaining before completing her plan and thus time to reconsider and perhaps decide not to ever follow through. **Answer C is not correct** because enrollment in the auto class would not to be a substantial enough act in furtherance of the crime. While jurisdictions vary as to the act requirement, virtually all require more than the merest preparation toward the commission of the murder. *United States v. Lee*, 603 F.3d 904 (11th Cir. 2010). Sally's enrollment would be too minor an act to qualify for an attempt conviction. Therefore, **Answer D is also incorrect**, because the only relevant inquiry is whether the act taken is mere preparation. **Answer A is wrong** because Sally's confession demonstrated her intent. The problem here relates to whether the act would be considered beyond mere preparation, not whether she had the requisite mental state.

53. **Yes.** There are two requirements for attempt liability: (1) act beyond mere preparation, as noted above, and (2) intent of the defendant that a crime be committed. The crime of attempt seeks to punish culpable individuals who have moved in the direction of committing a crime, coupled with a serious purpose to achieve that end. Lying in wait and getting ready to commit a crime would be viewed in most jurisdictions as evidence of substantial steps toward the commission of a crime, acts in close proximity to the commission of a crime. *United States v. Cooper*, 2022 WL 2526731 (D.D.C. 2022). They would, thus, satisfy the act requirement for the crime of attempt. Next, the government must also demonstrate that Sally intended to commit the crime. Sally's knowledge of her husband's affair, her enrollment in (and completion of) the auto course, and her presence at his work place would be sufficient evidence to show her intent.

54. **The best answer is B.** The crime of attempt requires intent. Sally may have acted recklessly, or with knowledge of the ramifications of her actions, allowing for a conviction of the crime of murder had her husband died. Her husband, however, did not die. Second degree murder is often defined as an unintentional killing committed in grossly reckless fashion. Attempt, however, requires a higher state of mind. Sally's mental state would not allow for a finding of attempt because she did not intend the killing. Therefore, she could not be convicted of attempted murder. *State v. Louis*, 384 P.3d 1 (Kan. 2016). As such, **answers C and D are incorrect. Answer A is wrong** because running a red light at such a high speed would likely be found to be sufficiently reckless under the law.

55. **Probably.** From Doug's actions, it seems the *mens rea* requirement of intent could be met in this case. The major question in Doug's prosecution will be whether he committed a sufficient act toward the completion of the crime. Very few states allow *any* act in furtherance to meet the act requirement for attempt. To do so might permit possibly innocent persons, and those with only vague or momentary criminal intentions, to be convicted of a crime without these people having genuinely committed themselves to the criminal enterprise. Most jurisdictions require that some significant act toward the commission of the intended crime be taken in order for one to be guilty of an attempted crime. This requirement ensures that culpable actions are punished, rather than bad thoughts alone. If the apartment were truly rented out for the purpose of facilitating the crime or the escape from the crime, Doug may have taken the necessary substantial step, particularly when it is coupled with the hiring of a safecracking expert. In addition, Doug was deterred from carrying out his plan only due to the actions of law enforcement and this will not aid in his resisting the attempt charge. Cal. Penal Code § 21a.

56. **The best answer is A.** The situation presented in this example could be best characterized as a case of factual impossibility. This argument has never been permitted as a defense. *People v. Dlugash*, 363 N.E.2d 1155 (N.Y. 1977). There would be no justification to allow this person to escape culpability because fortuity prevented the ultimate crime. Julia displayed her dangerousness to society very clearly, her act demonstrated this unequivocally, and had she been successful she would in fact have violated the law. **Answer B** does not truly deal with the impossibility issue, whereas **answer C** ignores entirely the issue. Julia took every act possible to ensure the killing would occur had it not been prevented by her own stupidity or mistake. Under the doctrine of factual impossibility, a defendant can be found guilty regardless of whether ultimate success was a real possibility. Thus, **answer D is not correct.**

57. **Answer B is the correct answer** if Julia genuinely thought she could commit the murder and took a substantial step toward that crime. Factual impossibility, as noted above, is no defense to the attempt charge. Therefore, **answer C is clearly wrong. Answer A is also wrong,** as most states do not allow *any* action to be the basis for the crime of attempt. Instead, the action must be substantial or major. **Answer D is incorrect,** as the elements of the attempt crime can be satisfied even if the elements of burglary can also be shown. There is no bar to charging the defendant with both crimes.

58. **Answer B is the best answer.** Yolanda's actions fulfill the requirements of attempt. **Answer A incorrectly** represents the purpose and scope of criminal law, for we do not punish individuals for bad thoughts alone. Individuals who act upon those bad thoughts, however, are prosecuted. Here, Yolanda may be convicted of attempted murder, because she not only wished her aunt to die, but took affirmative steps to fulfill that wish. Yolanda's decision to abandon her plan, after administering the pills, would not provide a defense to attempted murder. Thus, **answer C is not right.** Significantly, Yolanda did not

abandon her plan before the final step of giving her aunt the pills. Rather, it was only after she discovered her mistake, after the crime of attempt was already completed (when she would have successfully killed her aunt had there been no mistake on her part), that Yolanda changed her mind. No withdrawal is possible *after* the final criminal act has taken place. **Answer D is incorrect**, for it invokes again the concept of factual impossibility. Because her aunt would have died had Yolanda been correct as to the contents of the pills, it was a mere fortuity which prevented the killing. As such, it falls within the doctrine of factual impossibility, and that is no defense to an attempt charge.

CONSPIRACY

59. **The correct answer is A.** In a majority of states and in the federal system, a conspiracy to commit an offense does not merge with the substantive crime. *Pinkerton v. United States*, 328 U.S. 640 (1946). This means that Sybil and John can be convicted of both kidnapping and conspiracy to commit the kidnapping. The merger rule for conspiracy differs from attempt and solicitation, which generally do merge with the completed offenses. Thus **answer C is wrong.** This difference for conspiracy is based on the view that groups are more dangerous than individuals in terms of planning crimes. Moreover, merger is not mandated, as the very separate element of agreement needed for conspiracy is not present for the completed offense. **Answer B accurately reflects the rule in a minority of states**, which dictates that the charges for conspiracy and the substantive crime be merged. Most states and the federal system, though, do not follow this principle. **Answer D** states the common law rule where such a restriction as to punishment generally was not present; that is no longer the prevailing view.

60. The constitution would not be violated by sentencing Sybil and John for both the kidnapping and the conspiracy. The reference here would be to the double jeopardy protections of the Fifth and Fourteenth Amendments. But punishment for the conspiracy and a substantive crime does not violate these provisions in that each of the charges involves a distinct crime with separate elements. Conspiracy requites an agreement, while the substantive offense requires the completed act of kidnapping. *Pinkerton v. United States, supra.*

61. **Yes,** Gertie can still be convicted of conspiracy even though she was in jail at the time of the kidnapping and ransom request. As a matter of law, being put in jail is not a withdrawal from a conspiracy. *See United States v. Melton*, 131 F.3d 1400 (10th Cir. 1997). Generally, withdrawal depends on evidence of an affirmative act being taken by the defendant; the standard is the same even when the defendant is incarcerated. *See United States v. Alcorta*, 853 F.3d 1123 (10th Cir. 2017). Part of the reasoning for this is public policy: withdrawal exists as a defense to encourage defendants to stop the conspiracy and rat out their coconspirators. When a defendant is in jail without doing either of the aforementioned, she is not serving that policy goal.

62. **The correct answer is B.** Although no express agreement could be shown here, none is required for a conspiracy. The requisite agreement can be inferred from the circumstances. In fact, explicit agreements are rarely found in conspiracy prosecutions. Usually, conspiracy convictions have foundations in implied agreements, proven only with convincing circumstantial evidence. *Commonwealth v. Bell*, 2017 WL 1929043 (Pa. Super. 2017). Therefore, **answers A and C are incorrect.** Here, Lauren's complicity in Erika's actions could be inferred from their eye contact, by Lauren's inaction in the store, and the fact that they ran from the store together. A jury may find that her laughter signaled support for Erika's actions, and that in looking around, she was actually serving as a lookout. For these reasons, **answer D is also incorrect** because these circumstances could warrant a finding that Lauren acted out of an implicit understanding to rob the store.

63. **Answer C is the correct response,** as it accurately reflects the common law approach to the agreement element. Under this bilateral view, at least two people must agree to commit a criminal act to be found guilty of conspiracy. That is, at least two people must share a criminal intent. Without such a true agreement, Thomas is not guilty of conspiracy. **Answer A is clearly not right because** an actual agreement must exist for a conspiracy. Thomas's intent is not sufficient. **Answer B is also wrong** because it misstates the facts, as an agreement. **Answer D is incorrect** in that it presents a defense of factual impossibility. As with the crimes of attempt and solicitation, factual impossibly provides no defense to a conspiracy charge.

64. Thomas would be guilty of solicitation. With intent, he encouraged and aided Kate toward a crime.

65. Yes. The modern trend, based on the Model Penal Code, only requires that the person accused of conspiracy agree with another person. The government, under this view, need not show that any other person was in agreement. Therefore, Thomas can be convicted of conspiracy if he believed that he was acting pursuant to an understanding with Kate, even if Kate did not truly share his criminal intent. Under this so-called unilateral approach, it is no defense if the other party to the supposed agreement never intended to agree, is acquitted, or is immune from prosecution. Even though there was no genuine agreement here, the unilateral approach allows society to hold Thomas culpable for his actions and for his intent, under the circumstances as he believed them to be. *State v. Brown*, 2017 WL 3255245 (N.J. App. 2017).

66. **The correct answer is B.** The usual rule, as noted above, is that a true agreement must be shown as the basis for a conspiracy conviction. Beth's sale of the drugs to Joel does not fulfill the chief requirement for conspiracy, as there was no true agreement. Thus, **answer A is incorrect,** unless the case were brought in a jurisdiction following the "unilateral approach," as indicated above. Generally, the crime of conspiracy does not merge with the completed offense, so that should present no bar to conviction. For this reason,

answer C is wrong. Answer D is also not the right answer, because the defense of entrapment generally requires more of a government inducement than is present here, as discussed below.

67. Although it is possible that Zeb could be convicted of conspiracy on the indicated facts, it is unlikely without further evidence of his knowledge and intent. It may be difficult to prove that Zeb knew why Betty wanted the plastic bags. If there was further proof that Zeb was involved in the drug operation on a regular basis, a prosecutor might be able to demonstrate the required intent in that Zeb provided Betty the necessary information to make the sale that day. Without such proof that the boyfriend at least had knowledge of the transaction taking place, no agreement can be inferred from the circumstances. If Zeb had been in the room when Betty made the deal with Joel, for example, an agreement could be implied from the circumstances. In such a case, the requisite evidence would be in place to find the couple engaged in a conspiracy or a joint operation to sell drugs. While the government's case seems strong against Betty for sale of the drugs, without additional evidence, Zeb should escape a conviction for conspiracy.

The key here is that the government must prove that Zeb was aware that Betty was selling drugs and that he did something in furtherance of the crime. An agreement could then be inferred from the circumstances, but only because Zeb had knowledge of Betty's illegal activity. If knowledge could be shown, intent might be inferred from his offering of assistance. A jury could then conclude that Betty and Zeb had at least tacitly agreed to sell the drugs.

68. **The best answer is D.** While Karry's action in this transaction may lend itself to aiding and abetting more than a conspiracy charge, an agreement could be inferred from Karry's repeated sales to Reggie with the teenagers present. Unlike a one-time purchase, which may not allow such an inference to be drawn, under these circumstances, a fact-finder might conclude that Karry knew Reggie's intent. As she knew that he was to use the alcohol illegally, her tacit agreement to sell to him repeatedly could demonstrate her intent to make the sale. *Direct Sales Co. v. United States*, 319 U.S. 703 (1943). Therefore, **answer A is incorrect.** Moreover, **answer C is not the best answer** because intent can be found from circumstantial evidence. The facts here suggest that Karry might have wished to sell her merchandise to the teens, as long as the sale itself could be viewed as legitimate. Unless Karry can demonstrate she had no knowledge of Reggie's actions or intentions, it appears a fact finder could decide she intended the crime Reggie committed. **Answer B is not entirely true,** for if Karry did possess the knowledge that the crime be carried out, or intended that underage individuals could purchase alcohol from her through some means, she can be held criminally responsible.

69. **The best answer is D.** Conspiracy requires both the intent to agree to carry out an unlawful plan and an intent that the crime be committed. In general, criminal agents are responsible for the foreseeable ramifications of their actions. *Pinkerton v. United*

States, 328 U.S. 640 (1946). In this case, while it appears that the group had purposefully agreed to attack Marco, the prosecution would have to prove that the group intended to kill Marco for the charge of conspiracy to commit murder to be valid. The individual members of the group may have some criminal liability for murder or manslaughter, in that their actions may be found to be so reckless that they can be held responsible for Marco's death. But conspiracy to commit murder is a distinct offense requiring the intent to agree and the intent to kill. Because such intents could not be proven here, **answer B is wrong.**

Answer C is incorrect because the government likely could show that the group agreed to beat up Marco. As discussed above, an agreement can be inferred from the circumstances. **Answer A is not right** because the intent relates to an attack, not necessarily to a homicide. If the government was able to establish that the intent of the group was to kill Marco, then a conviction of conspiracy to commit murder would be possible. Yet, it is more likely that this group did not intend Marco's death, and only acted with a reckless disregard of the impact of their actions. As these answers show, the state of mind requirement for conspiracy can be higher than for the substantive criminal object of the conspiracy, precluding a conviction of conspiracy in some situations although the crime itself may have been committed while acting in concert with others.

70. **Yes.** The group likely will be convicted, as indicated above, because a fact finder could decide that the members of the group all agreed — even if not expressly — to physically harm Marco.

71. **The correct answer is B.** As long as Steve acted in furtherance of the conspiracy, and as long as those actions were foreseeable, the liability for those actions is attributed to Catherine unless she affirmatively withdrew, see below. The justification for this expansive liability rests on the foundation that conspiracy is intended to punish criminals acting in concert. In criminal law, people are held responsible for the full consequences of their actions, as long as those consequences can be seen as foreseeable results of the criminal activity. *Pinkerton v. United States*, 328 U.S. 640 (1946). In this situation, Steve's financial trouble and resulting expanded operations in the drug trade were clearly foreseeable. Thus, **answer C is wrong.** The network in place at the time of Steve's arrest seems a likely result of an addict managing a small-scale drug operation. **Answer A is not right** because Catherine's liability is limited to foreseeable, not all, consequences. Catherine's distance from the operation will not absolve her of liability as it is not sufficient to constitute withdrawal. For this reason, **answer D is incorrect.**

72. **The best answer is A.** Although Catherine's actions may not satisfy the requirements of abandonment for the crime of conspiracy, in most states, such withdrawal limits liability for later crimes. Therefore, **answers C and D are incorrect. Answer B is also incorrect**, as withdrawal is generally effective only if affirmative actions are taken in addition to notice. *People v. Navarro*, 497 P.3d 935 (Cal. 2021).

73. **The correct answer is B.** A conspirator will be held responsible for the conspiracy as long as any of its members perpetuate the conspiracy through the commission of an overt act. Any act, however minor, taken by any conspirator will keep the statute of limitations from running. *United States v. Payne*, 591 F.3d 46 (2d Cir. 2010). This demonstrates another way in which conspiracy law can have a wider scope in punishing culpable individuals than other areas of criminal law. **Answer A is an incorrect statement** of the operation of statutes of limitations. They provide a bar to prosecution if the required amount of time has elapsed. **Answer C is also wrong.** While it correctly states the law, it is inapplicable to this case, as actions were taken during the period. As explained above, **answer D is not right.** The scope of conspiracy liability extends beyond one individual in order to make all actors responsible for the foreseeable acts of others, even with regard to the use of the statute of limitations.

74. **Probably not.** Jalen may very well be convicted of murder if the killing is viewed as foreseeable under either an aiding and abetting theory or a conspiracy claim. Conviction for conspiracy to commit murder, however, seems highly unlikely. The joint action in the beating of Sheldon could give rise to an inference of an agreement to injure the victim. Jalen's intent to do harm to Sheldon is clear, but an intent to kill the victim by knifing him is not so apparent on Jalen's part. Jalen could be held responsible for the foreseeable criminal actions of his co-conspirator Cooper, which might include the killing. Neither Cooper nor Jalen can likely be convicted of conspiracy to commit murder, however, for the prosecution must prove that each intended to carry out an agreement to kill the victim at that time. The facts do not seem to support such a showing.

75. **Answer D is the correct answer.** If the prosecution is brought under one general conspiracy statute, the one agreement can only be the basis for one charge. *Braverman v. United States*, 317 U.S. 49 (1942). Therefore, both **answers A and B are incorrect.** Even with respect to those statutes that require overt acts (and federal drug conspiracy statutes generally do not), any act, however minimal, will suffice. Therefore, **answer C incorrect.**

76. **Answer B is the correct answer.** The Supreme Court has decided that the key constitutional focus is on the legislative intent to divide up responsibility for the two criminal acts, demonstrated here with the presence of distinct conspiracy statutes dealing with related activities. *Albernaz v. United States*, 450 U.S. 333 (1981). In that case, the Court held such a prosecution would not violate double jeopardy principles, thus making **answer D wrong.** The prosecution would be valid, even though a single agreement would form the basis for showing violations of two distinct statutes. **Answer A, therefore, would be incorrect, as would answer C.**

Crimes

THE PROPERTY OFFENSES:
LARCENY, EMBEZZLEMENT, FALSE PRETENSES

77. **The best answer is answer A.** Rodrigo met all of the requirements of larceny, including intent to steal. This intent could be demonstrated by all of his actions. The taking element is satisfied by the slightest movement away from the premises. *Barnett v. State Farm Ins. Co.*, 132 Cal. Rptr. 3d 742 (Cal. App. 2011). **Answer B is wrong** because while there was not a successful actual theft of the jacket, the taking element has been shown. Removing the goods at all from the owner's control whatsoever satisfies the offense requirement. As such, **answer D is incorrect. Answer C is also incorrect** because although Rodrigo had the store's consent in entering the store, that consent did not extend to theft. The trespass requirement does not allow those who have falsely gained consent of the owner for entrance to escape liability.

78. **The best answer is A.** Juanita was in "possession" of the plant, meaning that she had authority regarding the legitimate use and maintenance of the good, a key requirement for embezzlement. *People v. Gesch*, 2021 WL 4395273 (Mich. App. 2021). **Answer B is wrong**, as larceny involves a theft committed by someone not in possession, but only in mere custody, of the goods. **Answer C is also wrong** as title did not pass here (the rightful owner was not giving the plant to Juanita), an essential element of the crime of false pretenses. Although Juanita was the manager, she was not authorized to sell goods for her personal use. **Answer D is not correct,** as a robbery is defined as the taking of property by force or threat of force, not present here.

79. Amy's actions, while not larceny in the most usual sense, satisfy all of the required elements of that crime. The first element, trespass, is met; although Amy was invited onto the premises by the restaurant, it was on the condition that she would pay for her meal. Her conduct constitutes trespass. *Carter v. Commonwealth*, 694 S.E.2d 590 (Va. 2010). In eating her meal, she accomplished a taking and the asportation element could be considered met as she left the restaurant full of free food. The food was the personal property of the restaurant, as it only provided the meal on the condition that she would pay. Whether Amy had the intent to steal would be the most problematic element to prove. Increasingly, the law looks to the intent of the defendant at the time of the flight to determine whether there was a larceny committed. The common law focused on the intent to steal

at the time of the initial taking, here the eating. Amy, of course, did not have that intention at the start. However, the proper solution in such a situation is not to merely leave without payment, but to return to pay for the meal or to make other such arrangements. Once she decided to leave the restaurant without paying, Amy did form the intent to steal. Today, most courts would conclude that this action constitutes larceny.

80. **The correct answer is A.** The elements for embezzlement differ slightly from jurisdiction to jurisdiction, but returning the money will never be sufficient to absolve the defendant of liability. Once the money is taken and put to one's own use, the offense is complete. Another consistent element of embezzlement is that the defendant was in a fiduciary or trust relationship as to the property taken. *People v. Romanowski*, 391 P.3d 633 (Cal. 2017). As Thomas was able to appropriate the money for his own use by virtue of his employment relationship with the bank, his actions meet the criteria for embezzlement. Generally, the elements of embezzlement require such an employee relationship and the taking or fraudulent conversion—for however short a period—of the property of another, with the intent to deprive the owner of its use. Here, Thomas's actions met all of these requirements and, thus, he will likely be found guilty of embezzlement. Therefore, **answers B and D are incorrect.** In taking the money, Thomas was involved in the employment relationship even if he acted beyond the scope of his authority. Thus, **answer C is wrong.**

81. Intent forms one of the elements of embezzlement, but the intent to take or fraudulently convert property to one's own use (the state of mind needed for embezzlement) could be established by the circumstances. Luis knew he was not authorized to give these special favors to his friends rather than his clients. By giving favors to his friends, he intended to take profits and property from his employer. As such, **answer A is incorrect. Answer B is similarly flawed,** in that embezzlement often covers not only money but personal property as well. *People v. Viana*, 377 P.3d 805 (Cal. 2016). Moreover, while the phones were property, the discounted service resulted in fewer profits to the company, and the courts could consider this as lost money. For these reasons, **answer C is the best answer.** The statute in the jurisdiction will determine whether such action is considered embezzlement, but personal property is almost always included in embezzlement actions, in addition to money. **Answer D is incorrect** in that it suggests that the company decides whether a particular action is embezzlement. While the company will have some role in the prosecution, once the employee misconduct is brought to the attention of the public authorities, it is the government that must decide whether to bring criminal charges.

82. **The correct answer is C.** An individual cannot be guilty of embezzlement if they convert their own property. In order to qualify as embezzlement, it must involve the conversion of another's property. Therefore, contractors cannot be found guilty of embezzling funds received as a down payment because, upon receipt, the money becomes the legal property of the contractor. *State v. Kalinowski*, 460 P.3d 79 (N.M. App. 2019). As such, **answers A and B are not correct,** because even though Chris did not finish constructing the home, he was not in fraudulent possession of the $25,000 after he received the deposit. And **answer D is not correct** because there is no evidence of Chris's intent to complete the project.

83. **The best answer is B.** Lawrence made a false representation about the car being worth $15,000 and intended to deceive Teri in order to obtain the car, as evidenced by the faulty check. *State v. Hallum*, 783 S.E.2d 294 (N.C. App. 2016). **Answer A is not correct**, because there is no information to suggest that Lawrence lacked any knowledge of cars or is not a mechanic. Even if he is not, the relevant false representation is the one Lawrence made about the price of the car. **Answer C is not correct**, because the mere fact that Teri accepted the offer is a necessary, but not sufficient, requirement of the crime. And **answer D is not correct**, because foreseeability is not required to be found guilty of false pretenses.

84. **Answer A is the best answer.** By passing off plain white sneakers as the special sneakers the buyer requested, Daniel successfully made a false representation with the intent to deceive the buyer. *State v. Hallum*, 783 S.E.2d 294 (N.C. Ct. App. 2016). **Answer B is not correct** because whether Daniel knew the buyer would be deceived is not an element of obtaining money by false pretenses. **Answer C is not correct** because an individual does not escape liability simply because the person they are attempting to deceive failed to ask questions. And **answer D is incorrect** because the relevant inquiry is whether Daniel's false representation resulted in the buyer being deceived, not how long it took the buyer to realize he was deceived.

85. **The best answer is C.** False pretenses requires that the defendant *knowingly* misrepresent a past or present material fact with the *intent* to defraud. *Bohling v. State*, 388 P.3d 502 (Wyo. 2017). While Gary certainly would fit these requirements, Stephanie was unaware of the fraud. Therefore, Stephanie lacked the *mens rea* for false pretenses. Stephanie did misrepresent material facts and was engaged in deceiving investors, but she was unaware of the falsity of her statements. She may have been gullible, but Stephanie did not intend fraudulent action. **Answers A and B are incorrect** for this reason. **Answer D is also incorrect**, as the misrepresentation was of a past or present fact. Although the main misrepresentation here would clearly be the ultimate plan to construct a retirement community, the investors were convinced to participate based on the statements that the land had been purchased and roads had been constructed. While Stephanie will likely not be convicted due to her lack of the required state of mind, Gary could be found criminally responsible.

OFFENSES AGAINST THE HABITATION: BURGLARY, ARSON

86. **The best answer is answer A.** Under the common law definition of burglary, six elements must be met: (1) breaking, (2) entering, (3) at night, (4) in the dwelling house, (5) of another, (6) with intent to commit a felony inside. *People v. Fuentes*, 258 P.3d

320 (Colo. App. 2011). **Answer D is not correct,** as the law does not distinguish between early and late-night break-ins. Burglary involves more than a mere robbery in the home, so **answer B is not the best answer.** The breaking requirement demands the creation of some opening to gain entry, and in this case the perpetrator gained access with the homeowner's unwilling assistance. Courts have long recognized entry by threat to be a breaking, hence all the elements of the crime have been met. **Answer C, then, is incorrect.**

87. **Answer B is the best answer,** as the common law required a break-in at night. Thus, **answer A is wrong.** Most — but not all — modern statutes do not have a nighttime break-in element. Wis. Stat. §943.10. So, **answers C and D could be correct,** depending upon the jurisdiction.

88. **Yes.** Even though Bella co-owned the house and was still legally married to the victim, she can be deemed a burglar. "An owner can be properly convicted of burglarizing premises he [or she] owns but which are occupied by another." *People v. Novak*, 50 N.Y.S.3d 577 (N.Y. Sup. Ct. App. 2017).

89. **No.** The key requirements for arson include the malicious burning of the dwelling of another. While other persons' dwellings were burned here, it is unlikely that the malice requirement can be satisfied. Dave was certainly negligent in tossing the lit cigarette. Malice, however, normally involves an intentional or clearly foreseeable burning. *Harnden v. State*, 378 P.3d 611 (Wyo. 2016). Although Dave was foolish and unreasonable, he probably was not malicious. He is, therefore, not likely to be found guilty of arson.

90. **Answer D is the correct answer,** as arson under the common law requires some burning or flame of fire, however slight. Some modern statutes have expanded the common law definition by no longer requiring burning as an element of the crime; an explosion can be sufficient. 29 Ohio Rev. Code §2909.02. **Answer A is, then, incorrect. Answer B is wrong,** as no entry is needed for an arson, nor does the entire structure have to be destroyed. **Answer C is, therefore, also incorrect.** Fire is the key to arson. Without it here, the crime cannot be arson.

91. Nicolena committed the crime of attempted arson. With intent to burn the neighbor's house, she took a very substantial step toward that goal.

HOMICIDE

Killing

92. **The best answer is B.** Under the common law, a death must occur within one year and a day of the underlying event for the perpetrator to be found guilty of murder. The "year

and a day" rule originally existed because of problems in showing causation between an act and a death when a long period of time had elapsed. This rule creates an artificial limit on the ability to prove causation and assumes that a causal connection cannot be proven if the death occurs more than one year and one day after the act. While widely used in earlier days, the "year and a day" common law rule is rarely seen today. Because the question asks about the common law and Keesha died about one year and one month after Sam fired the shot, he cannot be convicted of murder under the common law. Thus, **Answer A is not correct.**

Murder does not necessarily require the intent to kill. Murder is the unlawful killing of another person with malice. Malice is established by: (1) the intent to kill; (2) the intent to inflict great bodily harm; (3) gross recklessness (implied malice); or, (4) the waiver of malice because the death occurred during the commission of a felony (felony murder). Sam intended to inflict great bodily harm. On this basis, Sam could be found to have malice sufficient for him to be found guilty of murder. La. R.S. § 14:30. However, as with **answer A, answer C is incorrect** because the "year and a day" rule cuts off liability even where the requisite mental state and causation exist. **Answer D is not right.** Criminal law operates under the assumption that sane people can commit heinous acts. The mere fact that Sam shot Keesha is insufficient to establish an insanity defense.

93. Most states have eliminated the common law rule of "a year and a day." In those states, the causal relationship between an act and a death must still be proven, which often will become more difficult as time passes. Nonetheless, the mere number of days that elapsed between the date Keesha was shot and the day she died would not preclude conviction of Sam for murder in states that have rejected the common law rule. As stated by the Supreme Court in *Rogers v. Tennessee*, 532 U.S. 451, 462–63 (2001):

> The year and a day rule is widely viewed as an outdated relic of the common law.... [A]s practically every court recently to have considered the rule has noted, advances in medical and related science have so undermined the usefulness of the rule as to render it without question obsolete.

94. **Answer A is the best answer.** Murder is the unlawful killing of a person with malice. Killing is causing another person's death. It is impossible to kill a person who is already dead. Because John was already dead when Jane shot him, she did not cause his death and could not be found guilty of John's murder. *People v. Dlugash*, 363 N.E.2d 1155 (N.Y. 1977).

Whether Jane's actions may or may not have been sufficient to kill John if he had been alive is irrelevant. Because John was already dead, Jane could not have killed him under any circumstances. The unlawful killing of another person with malice is one of the basic elements of the crime of murder. For this reason, **answers B and C are not correct.** **Answer D is not the best answer because** the elements of the crime of murder have not been established. Although Jane had the intent to kill, she did not commit the act necessary for murder.

95. Although she cannot be convicted of murder, Jane committed the crime of attempted murder, as she intended to kill John and took the last possible step to achieve this goal. *People v. Dlugash*, 363 N.E.2d 1155 (N.Y. 1977).

96. **Answer D is the best answer.** According to the common law, a baby must be born alive to be considered a person under the law of homicide. *Keeler v. Superior Court*, 470 P.2d 617 (Cal. 1970). Because the crime of murder involves the killing of a person, William cannot be convicted of the baby's death if it was not born alive. This rule, which evolved during a period when it was difficult to discern the cause of a fetus's death, stated that a person could not be found guilty of murdering a fetus. Although William's intentions and actions would have been enough for him to be convicted of murder if the baby was born alive, those same actions and intentions would not be sufficient to convict William of murder if the baby was born dead. Although William had the intent to kill, he did not commit the act of killing under the common law. Life does not begin until birth under the common law, so William did not kill a person. Therefore, **answer A is incorrect. Answer B is not right** because the timing of the act in relation to the birth is irrelevant. In the scenario in which the baby is born alive and then dies a short time after, the important inquiry is whether a causal connection can be made between the act and the death, even if that act occurred before the baby's birth. **Answer C is not correct** because it does not distinguish between the two fact patterns. A causal connection must always be established between an act and a death to establish the crime of murder. The common law rule assumes that the death of a fetus was not the result of the act. For this reason, if a baby is born dead, any act that occurred prior to the child's birth cannot be an element of the crime of murder. If, however, the baby is born alive and dies later — even mere moments later — William may be convicted of murder if that prior act caused the baby's death.

97. **Yes.** Feticide statutes make the killing of a fetus illegal. In states that have enacted such laws, it would be possible for William to be convicted of the murder of a fetus based on harm caused to the fetus *in utero* regardless of whether the baby is born alive and dies shortly thereafter or is stillborn. Ind. Code § 35-42-1.

98. **Answer C is the best answer.** At common law, death was defined as the cessation of respiratory and cardiac function. Thus, under the common law, James would not have been considered dead when the doctors removed his life support. Under modern statutes, however, death is defined as the irreversible cessation of either circulatory and respiratory functions or of all functions of the entire brain. Because James was legally dead at the time his life support was removed, the doctors could not be considered an intervening cause of his death. Under modern statutes, James's death would be the result of the act that caused the trauma, which was the car accident.

Although **answer A would be the best answer** under the common law, death has been statutorily redefined in the modern statutes as noted above. While it may be tempting to say that the doctors hastened James's death, modern statutes define death as brain death. Because James was legally dead when the doctors disconnected the life support, **answer B is not correct. Answer D is not the best answer.** If a car accident is caused by truly reckless behavior, it may well be the basis of an involuntary manslaughter or even murder, as discussed below.

Murder

99. **Answer A is the best answer.** An act that causes death must be committed with malice in order for a person to be convicted of murder. As noted above, malice is defined as: (1) the intent to kill; (2) the intent to commit serious bodily injury; (3) gross recklessness (implied malice); or (4) a crime committed during the commission of a felony. The malice element of murder can be established by an act that creates a very high probability of death or serious bodily injury. *Brinkley v. State*, 233 A.2d 56 (Del. 1967). Driving at extremely high speeds creates a great probability of death. On this basis, Amy could be found guilty of murder. Driving over the speed limit but at lower speeds may be unreasonably risky, which could result in a charge of involuntary manslaughter.

   Answer B is not correct because prior intent that has been abandoned is not relevant to an act that occurs later. Although malice can be implied from Amy's reckless behavior, it cannot be satisfied from an abandoned intent to kill. Bess did not have control over the car after Amy began speeding. When Bess got into the car, she did not know that Amy was going to drive at dangerously high speeds. She did not voluntarily expose herself to the extreme danger and was not free to get out of the car once the car was speeding down the road. Thus, **answer C is wrong. Answer D is not correct** because Amy knew that driving that fast was extremely dangerous; in fact, she was driving fast because she found the danger exhilarating. As Amy knew that her behavior was extremely risky, malice can be shown by gross recklessness.

100. **Answer C is the best answer.** At common law, an omission is normally not criminal. Under most circumstances, the criminal law does not require strangers to act on behalf of others. A failure to act is only criminal under the common law when a legal duty to act exists. Such a legal duty to act can be created by statute or by contract. *Commonwealth v. Pestinikas*, 617 A.2d 1339 (Pa. Sup. Ct. 1992). Because Michael entered into an employment contract to take care of Jolinda, he can be held criminally liable for his failure to care for her. Hence, **answer A is incorrect.**

   A failure to act can be the cause of death as much as an affirmative act. Where there is a duty, the failure to act fulfills the *actus reus* element of the crime, and no overt act is required. **Answer B is incorrect** because the law only punishes those with a duty to act in such circumstances. Michael's failure to act, in violation of his legal duty to act, was the cause of Jolinda's malnutrition that resulted in her death. An omission to act is not criminal where only a moral duty to act, and not a legal duty, exists. Societal norms do not define the elements of a crime. **Answer D is wrong** because Michael's failure to act on a moral duty does not make him a criminal. Here, Michael can be found criminally liable only because of his legal duty to act, not because he had a moral obligation to care for Jolinda.

101.   Murder is an illegal killing with malice. The clearest way to demonstrate malice is the intent to kill. Here, Leonard acted out of his intent to kill the woman upstairs. He knew that telling the woman that her daughter was dead would be a terrible shock and would probably kill her due to her heart condition. Although the heart attack was the precise cause of her death, Leonard's words are the legal cause of her death. By uttering those words, he instigated the heart attack. Even an act as small as saying a few words can be the cause of death, so long as malice can be established. Leonard's planning demonstrates premeditation and deliberation. On this basis, he can be found guilty of first degree murder, as explored below.

102.   **The best answer is answer B.** For the crime of murder, the government must show an intent to kill, an intent to commit serious bodily injury, gross recklessness, or that a killing occurred during the commission of a felony. Under this definition, it is unlikely that a jury could find that Abdul committed murder. Because it would be possible for Abdul to be convicted of murder, even if he did not intend to kill Eric, **answer A is not the best answer.** As explained above, if a jury found that Abdul had the intent to commit serious bodily injury, he could be convicted of murder.

   Answer C is incorrect because, based on the facts, it does not appear that Abdul intended to commit serious bodily injury to Eric. Instead, Abdul was just caught up in the excitement. He did not intend to seriously injure anyone, just give a few black eyes. A finding of malice based upon the intent to commit serious bodily injury must be more than an intent to inflict some injury. An intent to simply injure that unexpectedly causes death would result in a conviction for involuntary manslaughter, not murder. The gross recklessness element is also called a "depraved heart" or "malignant heart" murder. Gross recklessness is behavior so dangerous that it demonstrates a disregard for life; however, it does not have to be behavior that is almost certain to cause death. Still, merely reckless behavior is insufficient to establish the malice element required for murder. Because **answer D misstates** the recklessness requirement for murder, it is not the correct answer.

103.   The result might well change with these new facts. Normally people engaged in a fight which results in death are acting with some recklessness or negligence resulting in a conviction of, at most, either involuntary manslaughter or negligent homicide. When, however, the defendant is so large and is so well trained in fighting, he may be charged with knowledge of the extreme risk his fighting entails. A trier of fact could, then, find that his participation in a brawl constitutes gross recklessness allowing for a conclusion that he killed the victim with implied malice. He could be convicted, on this basis, of murder. *State v. Bias*, 195 S.E.2d 626 (W. Va. 1973).

104. **Answer B is the best answer.** Murder is the unlawful killing of another person with malice. Intent to kill, intent to commit great bodily harm, gross recklessness (implied malice), and felony murder are the four ways to establish the mental state for murder. Arturo did not intend to kill or to commit great bodily harm, and he was not being reckless. The only remaining way to establish murder would be felony murder. Felony murder is an unlawful killing that occurs during the commission of a violent felony. Or. Rev. Stat. § 163.115. Because larceny of a backpack is not a violent felony, Arturo cannot be found guilty of felony murder. Although Arturo did not intend to hit and kill the student, intent to kill is only one of four ways to establish the requisite mental state for murder. Because answer A only addresses this one possibility, **answer A is not the best answer.** In most jurisdictions, a crime is not complete until the criminal has reached a place of safety. In these circumstances, most jurisdictions would consider the school's parking lot to be part of the crime scene. Arturo would not be considered to be in a place of safety. If Arturo had committed a violent felony in the school, hitting a pedestrian in the parking lot might have been viewed as a killing during the commission of a violent felony, which would be a felony murder. Larceny of a backpack is not a violent felony, however, so **answer C is not correct.** Hitting the student while driving at a slow speed does not constitute gross recklessness. **Answer D is incorrect** because accidents can and do happen. Not all incidents involving an automobile hitting a person are necessarily the result of gross recklessness.

105. **Answer C is the best answer.** A killing committed during the commission of a violent felony is felony murder. The definition of a violent, or inherently dangerous, felony varies by jurisdiction. Some statutes list the specific felonies that can be used to establish felony murder. Other statutes simply use language such as "inherently dangerous offences," "forcible felonies," or "violent crimes." Under either approach, armed robbery would certainly be considered sufficient. Therefore, a killing committed during the commission of armed robbery would be a felony murder. Because malice is assumed, it does not matter that Arturo hit the student accidentally. Therefore, **answer A is not correct.** A crime is not completed until the criminal has reached a place of safety. The thief in this circumstance was not out of danger at the point in which he was driving from the school's parking lot. Because the armed robbery was still being committed as he fled, Arturo hit the student during the commission of the felony, not after. *People v. Johnson*, 7 Cal. Rptr. 2d 23 (Cal. App. 1992). For this reason, **answer B is wrong.** Although the student died as a result of being hit by Arturo's car, that fact alone is not sufficient to establish murder. As a consequence, **answer D is not the best answer.** A person who is hit and killed by a carefully driven vehicle, an accident that occurred in the absence of a dangerous crime or felony, would ordinarily not be a victim of murder because the defendant's *mens rea* would be lacking.

106. Liability for the actions of others during the commission of an inherently dangerous felony varies considerably by jurisdiction. On one end of the spectrum, a felon can only be liable in some states if he is the person who directly caused the death ("pulled the trigger"). The rationale underlying this approach is that a person is responsible only for his own acts and that a person should not be held responsible for an act in opposition to his purposes. Under this approach, Matt would not be liable for the bystander's death under a felony murder theory because he did not directly cause the death. States adopting "but for" causation fall at the other end of the spectrum. The rationale underlying this approach is that the felon created the dangerous situation and should be held accountable for any deaths resulting from the situation. Under this approach, Matt would be liable for the bystander's death because, but for the crime Matt committed and the fact that he was fleeing while a policeman was chasing him at gunpoint, the bystander would not have been killed. Many jurisdictions fall somewhere between these two approaches, using a traditional proximate cause test to determine liability, focusing on the foreseeability of the resulting death. *People v. Matos*, 634 N.E.2d 157 (N.Y. 1994). Under this test, Matt likely would be found guilty.

107. Almost certainly, in virtually all jurisdictions, Matt will be held criminally responsible for the death of the hostage. Such an action is incredibly dangerous, and foreseeability of great harm to the hostage is quite clear. Most courts would, then, find felony murder here when the felon has taken the additional step of exposing an innocent person to such a high risk. *Jackson v. State*, 408 A.2d 711 (Md. 1979). To be sure, even without a felony murder charge, Matt would very likely be found guilty of murder with a determination that his actions were grossly reckless (implied malice).

108. **The best answer is answer A.** In most states, the crime upon which the felony murder rule is predicated must be independent of the felony resulting in homicide. *People v. Chun*, 203 P.3d 425 (Cal. 2009). If the felony directly resulting in the homicide were permitted to be the underlying felony, then any assault that resulted in death could be "bumped up" to murder using the assault as the basis for the felony murder. An assault that occurs during a robbery is done with an independent purpose (stealing property), so the robbery can be used as a basis for felony murder. Here, the assault was done with the purpose of physically harming Avi, so there is no independent purpose for the actions that caused the death. For this reason, the assault cannot be used as the basis for felony murder in most states. Although the assault is a dangerous felony, it is merged with the homicide, so **answer C is incorrect.**

Answer B is not correct because the ability to convict on alternate grounds of malice does not preclude the use of the felony murder rule. Often, a person convicted using the felony murder rule could have been convicted by demonstrating malice instead. The felony murder rule provides a shortcut for the prosecution; instead of having to prove malice, which can be difficult, the prosecution must prove only that a dangerous felony occurred and that the homicide occurred during the commission of that felony. Although it is true that "the felony murder rule eliminates the need to demonstrate malice," this statement is not responsive to the question. **Answer D is, therefore, not the best answer.**

109. Felony murder involves a killing that occurs during the commission of a dangerous felony. Because Ronald and Janie were still at the scene of the arson, the killings clearly occurred during the commission of dangerous felony. Jurisdictions differ as to how they approach liability both for killings by co-felons and for killings by third parties. Ronald did not directly commit either murder, so guilt would have to be imputed to him as a party to the crime. Janie would have been guilty of murdering the bystander, so Ronald would be guilty as a co-felon for this foreseeable killing.

Ronald may not, in some states, be found guilty as to Janie's death, however, under the felony murder rule. In states adopting one extreme approach, a felon is not liable — under the rule — for killings committed by third parties. *Smith v. Myers*, 261 A.2d 550 (Pa. 1970). Ronald would not be held accountable — with a felony murder theory — for the death of his partner in such states because the police officer was acting in opposition to the purposes of the crime. In states adopting a contrary approach, a felon is responsible for all foreseeable killings that occur during the commission of the felony no matter who directly causes the deaths. *Jackson v. State*, 408 A.2d 711 (Md. 1979). Because it was foreseeable that Ronald, Janie, or another person could have been killed during the arson, Ronald would be guilty of the felony murder of Janie in states adopting the foreseeable killings approach, even though neither he nor his co-felon pulled the trigger that caused the bystander's death.

110. Jamie and Ronald's actions were extremely dangerous, creating a tremendous risk of harm to others. As a consequence, they would likely both be convicted of the two murders under an implied malice theory because they were grossly reckless.

111. **The correct answer is A.** In a felony murder prosecution, the government is relieved of its duty to generally prove a high state of mind as to the killing because of the danger created by the commission of the underlying violent felony. Still, the felony murder theory can only proceed if that underlying violent felony has been proved beyond a reasonable doubt, even if that crime is not separately charged. *People v. Croy*, 710 P.2d 392 (Cal. 1985). Hence, **answers C and D are incorrect. Answer B is wrong**, as it deals with the harmless error rule, a principle only involved when an error was committed by the trial court.

112. **Answer A is the best answer.** Under the modern law in many jurisdictions, murder is divided into degrees. First degree murder requires the intent to kill, and also premeditation and deliberation. Mich. Comp. Laws § 750.316. Based on Hannibal's statement, a jury could determine that he intended to kill his victims, and that he killed them with deliberation and after premeditation. On this basis, Hannibal can be found guilty of first degree murder.

Second degree murder is a lesser included offense of first degree murder. That is, first degree murder contains all the elements of second degree murder, and also the added elements of premeditation and deliberation. By removing those two elements, second degree murder is defined as an unlawful killing with malice aforethought. **Answer B is not the best answer** because Hannibal, in addition to committing these murders with malice, fulfilled the added elements included in the offense of first degree murder, premeditation and deliberation. For the same reason, **answer C is not the best answer.** Although Hannibal satisfied each of the elements required for a conviction for second degree murder, a conviction for first degree murder is more appropriate because he killed with premeditation and deliberation.

Answer D is not correct. Voluntary manslaughter truly is murder—based upon an intentional killing—but reduced due to the added "heat of passion" element. Hannibal cannot claim to have acted in the heat of passion as it is, by definition, an immediate response to serious provocation. Because Hannibal carefully planned the murders, he did not act in the heat of passion and his killings cannot be viewed as voluntary manslaughter.

113.   **Answer A is the best answer.** First degree murder, by statute, often involves the unlawful killing of a person with malice aforethought, plus premeditation and deliberation. Lien planned the murder for more than a year, so she had plenty of time to consider and reconsider her actions. Given the circumstances in this case, it appears that Lien acted with malice aforethought (satisfied here by an intent to kill), premeditation, and deliberation. Because the intent to kill, in and of itself, is not sufficient for a conviction of first degree murder, **answer B is not correct.**

Particularly gruesome and heinous homicides are usually first degree murders. The rationale is that the defendant must have had time to consider her actions during the course of the murder. For example, one may intend to kill and stab a person all in a few seconds. To kill a person by carving him up into little pieces takes considerably more time. A person who commits such a crime clearly had time to think about what she was doing during the commission of the crime. Nonetheless, not all first degree murders are gruesome or heinous. First degree murder only requires that the defendant have formed an intent to kill and then deliberated and premeditated on it. For this reason, **answer C is wrong.**

Second degree murder is the unlawful killing of a person with malice aforethought (but without premeditation and deliberation). Second degree murder is the "typical" type of murder; most murders fall into this category. Intent to kill is one way of demonstrating the mental state for second degree murder. In this case, Lien had the intent to kill. For that reason, she had the mental state to be convicted of second degree murder. However, because she planned the murder ahead of time, the prosecution could show the added elements of premeditation and deliberation necessary for a conviction for first degree murder. Although Lien could be convicted of second degree murder, **answer D is not the best answer. Answer A is the more complete answer**, and the best answer applied to these facts, because it includes the elements of both first degree and second degree murder, elements that Lien satisfied.

114. The proposed jury instruction illustrates clearly the great but unresolved debate found in courts throughout the United States regarding the evidence necessary to demonstrate the mental state for the crime of first degree murder. Some courts emphasize that the time factor is insignificant, that the real question concerns whether the defendant thoughtfully considered his actions prior to killing. For these courts, the instruction would be proper, as it would demonstrate to the jurors that reflection by the defendant was the important issue, not the time frame for the killing. *Kirby v. Commonwealth*, 653 S.E.2d 600 (Va. App. 2007). Other courts, however, take quite a different view. They conclude that allowing a finding of premeditation and deliberation based on actions that took place mere moments apart obscures the distinction between the two degrees of murder. They would require considerably more proof to show true considered decision-making by the defendant in killing the victim. *State v. Horn*, 750 S.E.2d 248 (W. Va. 2013).

115. **Answer B is the best answer.** The *corpus delicti* of a crime is the "body of the crime." This phrase is usually referred to when there is a problem demonstrating that a crime has actually occurred, such as when the body of a person suspected to be killed is not recovered. To demonstrate that a death was the result of murder, the prosecution must establish the basic elements of the crime: an unlawful act done with malicious intent that caused the death of a person. All elements of a crime can be proven beyond a reasonable doubt using purely circumstantial evidence. Given the circumstantial evidence in this case, including the fact that Juanita purchased a large insurance policy on Bill's life and that Bill has not been heard from since he left for his trip with Juanita, the elements of the crime of murder could be shown in this case, even if Bill's body is never recovered. Hence, **answer D is not correct.**

Answer A is not the best answer because it does not establish an element of the crime of murder. Motive alone is insufficient to prove a causal relationship between a death and a defendant. There must be enough evidence to prove the elements of the crime of murder (i.e., the killing of a person, with malice aforethought) beyond a reasonable doubt.

In criminal law, the *mens rea* of intent is almost always proven by circumstantial evidence because no one can know for certain what the defendant intended. Generally, the trier of fact considers the evidence and determines that the only reasonable explanation for the defendant's actions is that she intended to do what she did. In the same way, the *actus reus* can also be proven by circumstantial evidence. In this case, the prosecution will show that the only reasonable explanation for Bill's disappearance is that he is dead. Based in part upon such an analysis, Juanita can be convicted of murder. A body is not required to prove beyond a reasonable doubt that a death has occurred if such circumstantial evidence exists. *State v. Keadle*, 977 N.W.2d 207 (Neb. 2022). Therefore, **answer C is incorrect.**

Manslaughter

116. **Voluntary manslaughter.** This crime may be viewed as a murder, but one committed in the "heat of passion." Voluntary manslaughter occurs when there is said to be a sudden provocation serious enough that it would cause a reasonable person to act in the same violent way as the defendant did. *People v. Beltran*, 301 P.3d 1120 (Cal. 2013). In such cases, the prosecution will prove all of the elements of murder with an intentional killing. While the defendant need not offer any evidence, normally the defense will introduce credible evidence showing that the crime was committed in the heat of passion, as here. The government would be able to demonstrate beyond a reasonable doubt that Pablo stabbed Sam with the intent either to kill him or to inflict great bodily harm to him. Without facts indicating heat of passion and adequate provocation, then, the crime here would be second degree murder. The showing of going "berserk" in response to the argument would, however, likely prove the element necessary for voluntary manslaughter.

117. In most jurisdictions, Pablo would now be found guilty of murder rather than voluntary manslaughter. The latter crime requires a showing of an intentional killing done *suddenly* in the heat of passion, caused by adequate provocation. The factor of suddenness is taken seriously by most decision-makers. *Phelps v. State*, 167 N.E.3d 685 (Ind. App. 2021). They are willing to determine that reasonable people might, in the moment, take regrettable actions making them less culpable. If those same people, however, are able to reflect on the situation, the view of lower culpability vanishes. Suddenness is generally required for the crime of voluntary manslaughter.

118. **Answer C is the best answer.** Although the criminal laws generally do not require one to act in aid of another, certain individuals may have a legal duty to take affirmative actions to assist others by virtue of their personal relationships. Under the common law, a duty of care was limited to very few relationships (e.g., parent/child, master/servant). *People v. Rolon*, 73 Cal. Rptr. 3d 358 (Cal. App. 2008). Because Anna was a small child and Tim was her father, Tim was obligated to seek medical attention when his daughter became very ill. **Answer A is wrong** because it applies the general rules of criminal law without considering the special relationship between Tim and his daughter that creates a duty to act.

Answer B is not correct because it does not accurately explain Tim's motives. Tim put off going to the doctor for financial reasons even when he knew his daughter needed medical attention. To withhold medical assistance for financial reasons exposed Tim's daughter to a substantial risk without reasonable justification. On this basis, Tim exhibited gross recklessness because he knew that keeping Anna at home was putting her in danger.

Voluntary manslaughter has, essentially, the same elements as murder but also "heat of passion," as explained above. **Answer D is not correct** because a lack of financial resources is not a legally adequate provocation. Acts taken in the heat of passion must be done in response to sudden, shocking provocation and must be the sort of response that an ordinary person might make. Alaska Stat. § 11.41.115. Because no such sudden provocation occurred here, and because most individuals would not respond to financial hardship by refusing to bring their very sick child to the doctor, Tim's actions cannot be seen as arising in the heat of passion.

119.   **Answer D is the best answer,** for murder can be based on such extreme risk being consciously taken by a defendant, even without any sort of intentional misconduct. *People v. Holmes*, 2013 WL 4033789 (Colo. Dist. Ct. 2013). With his own observations and the advice from the doctor, Tim may be viewed as having acted with gross recklessness, satisfying the "implied malice" requirement for murder. For that reason, **answers A and B are wrong. Answer C is not right** because without the information from the doctor it is not likely that a trier of fact would conclude that the risk was sufficiently great as to constitute murder rather than involuntary manslaughter. It should be noted, though, that the distinction between the two crimes is not well defined, and courts and juries have considerable leeway in this area in terms of the proof presented.

120.   Involuntary manslaughter is a homicide committed in a reckless fashion. *Commonwealth v. Curtis*, 174 N.E.3d 333 (Mass. App. 2021). Jerome hit the man with the intent to kill or harm. The intent does not have to exist far in advance; it may be formed only moments before acting. Jerome clearly stated that his intent was to kill the man; therefore, he is not guilty of involuntary manslaughter.

Voluntary manslaughter is an intentional killing done in the heat of passion, in response to a sudden adequate provocation. At common law, words alone were generally not enough to constitute adequate provocation in order to reduce murder to voluntary manslaughter. Some states still follow this rule. *Smith v. Commonwealth*, 821 S.E.2d 543 (Va. 2018). In those jurisdictions, Jerome would be guilty of murder. He would not be allowed to assert that the act was done in the heat of passion because, as a matter of law, words could not have provoked a reasonable person to kill. Jerome would have had to walk in on his wife and the man together or have had some sort of proof other than mere words to be able to claim that the murder was done in the heat of passion in response to adequate provocation.

Other states find that words alone may be sufficient to provoke a person to kill. In most of those jurisdictions that allow words alone, the courts consider whether or not there is sufficient evidence to show that a reasonable person would have been incited to kill in a hot-blooded passion. The evidence may be acts, acts and words, or words alone. In those jurisdictions, the murder could be reduced to a conviction of voluntary manslaughter. *People v. Najera*, 41 Cal. Rptr. 3d 244 (Cal. App. 2006).

121.   **B is the best answer.** Involuntary manslaughter is an unlawful killing resulting from a reckless disregard for human life. The defendant must be aware of the risk, as Malik was here. The degree of risk is less than that required for murder, seen as great or gross

recklessness. There are no clear lines, but courts have defined recklessness in many different ways, such as wanton disregard for human life, an indifference to consequences, or a taking of a risk that likely could result in *serious* harm or death. *Commonwealth v. Dragotta*, 71 N.E.3d 502 (Mass. 2017).

In most states, vehicular homicide resulting from some physical ailment or defect (e.g., drowsiness or vertigo caused by medication or alcohol, epilepsy) is usually involuntary manslaughter. Although people are aware of the risks involved, they do not expect it to happen to them. For the act to be successfully prosecuted as murder, it must be a *grossly* reckless act so likely to result in serious harm or death that the defendant virtually intended that result. Driving under the influence of medication does not rise to this level of risk; therefore, **answer A is not the best answer.**

Common tort negligence is based on the notion that a reasonable person would have known of the risk. Here the defendant was warned multiple times and had noticed how drowsy he became while taking the medicine. His later actions show a conscious disregard for safety and constitute reckless endangerment of the lives of others. Malik's behavior far exceeds mere negligence, so **answer C is not correct.**

Although it may not have been likely that the driver of the other car would be killed at such low speeds, Malik knew that driving a car in his condition could result in the death of himself or another driver. The exact scenario which results in death does not have to be foreseeable. It is enough that it was foreseeable that Malik's driving was likely to result in serious injury or death. Therefore, **answer D is not the best answer.**

KIDNAPPING

122. **The best answer is B.** Kidnapping consists of the unlawful confinement or removal of another, without consent, from that person's location of choice. Me. Stat. tit. 17-A § 301. Even a short distance away is sufficient to constitute a kidnapping, so **answer C is wrong.** *People v. Williams*, 212 Cal. Rptr. 3d 728 (Cal. App. 2017). **Answer A is not correct** because kidnapping only occurs if there is some confinement or movement against the will of the victim. The crime can be committed with the use of force, or the threatened use of force. Therefore, **answer D is also not correct.**

123. **The best answer is A,** as the force or threat of force need not be directed to any specific person for the crime of kidnapping to occur. *State v. Elenes-Rocha*, 85 Wash. App. 1020 (Wash. App. 1997). **Answer C, then, is incorrect. Answer B is not right**, as some force or threat of force is normally needed to satisfy the elements of the crime of kidnapping. For that reason, **answer D is also not right.**

124. **The best answer is C.** The time frame for the confinement is irrelevant, so long as the defendant is moved against his will, as in this case. *Reyes v. State*, 491 S.W.3d 36 (Tex.

Crim. App. 2016). **Answer A, therefore, is incorrect, as is answer B,** for the crime never requires any physical injury to be sustained by the victim. As indicated above, the crime is complete with the victim's confinement or movement, not with the threat. **Answer D is also incorrect.**

125. **Yes,** the kidnapping was complete when Dr. Rodriguez remained in the office against her will. While Travis will raise a number of serious challenges in response to the prosecution, none will succeed. In this case, the dentist was forced to remain in the room. She was not required to move to another location, which generally occurs in kidnappings. Kidnapping, however, involves either the removal of the victim or her confinement. The fact that the confinement took place in a familiar area is of no import. The key to the crime is that the defendant has forced the victim to move, or not move, against her will. Finally, the fact that the confinement was limited to a five- or ten-minute period does not matter. Any period of unlawful movement or confinement is sufficient for the purpose of the crime of kidnapping. While some modern statutes have degrees of the crime, linked to the time of the movement or confinement, these laws do not usually redefine the crime. They simply alter the punishment depending on the seriousness of the offense.

ROBBERY

126. **The correct answer is B.** In order to meet the requirements for a robbery, the defendant must take another's property from that person by violence or intimidation. *Gray v. United States*, 155 A.3d 377 (D.C. App. 2017). Regardless of whether the defendant would have been able to harm the victim, that element has been met if the victim in fact reasonably believed harm was likely. Therefore, **answers C and D are incorrect.** Robbery requires more than a larceny (i.e., simply taking property) and is punishable by a lengthier sentence. **Answer A is incorrect** for this reason. Robbery is considered more serious than larceny because it is a crime against both property and person, as it involves the use or threat of violence against a victim.

127. Patricia is not likely to be found guilty of robbery. Robbery is a serious crime against the person, not simply a property offense. As such, it requires a showing of force or threat of force directed against a victim. Given the seriousness of this element, the punishment for robbery is normally considerably greater than for theft offenses. Because a pickpocket usually takes property without notice, as opposed to using or threatening to use force against a victim, a pickpocket generally does not commit the crime of robbery.

128. Robbery requires that an individual intend to permanently deprive another of their property *at the time* they took it. *People v. DePriest*, 163 P.3d 896 (Cal. 2007). Because Peter intended to keep Nate's watch when he took it, **answer B is the best choice. Answer A is not the best answer** because, while the use of force is necessary for robbery, it

is not sufficient. Peter's intent to deprive Nate of his watch could have arisen after the use of force, but that would have amounted to, at most, theft. *People v. Jackson*, 376 P.3d 528 (Cal. 2016). **Answer C is not correct** because actual harm is not required to effectuate a robbery, just the use of force or fear. And **answer D is not correct** because, even though Peter attempted to return the watch, the relevant inquiry is his intent at the time of the act, not afterwards.

SEX OFFENSES

129. **Answer C is the best answer.** At common law, and in most statutes today, the crime of rape consists of sexual intercourse by force or threat of force with no consent by the victim. The forced entry of Emil inside Tina's body, without any indication of approval by Tina, would be sufficient to show no consent by her to the act. *Commonwealth v. Torres*, 57 N.E.3d 1065 (Mass. App. 2016). **Answer D is wrong**, because the consent need not be express so long as some indication is given that the consent is voluntary. In a situation such as this, silence of the victim typically is insufficient to show consent and some indication of assent must be demonstrated. Thus, **answer B is incorrect. Answer A is also incorrect** as it is not enough for the defendant to show that he did not realize there was a lack of approval of the act. The prosecution will succeed if the government shows that the victim did not consent, as is the case here.

130. At common law, many states required a specific threat or use of force to be shown for a conviction for the crime of rape. That is no longer the law in most jurisdictions. The forced entry of Emil inside Tina's body, under circumstances that would cause any reasonable person to be terrified, would likely constitute the use of force in most jurisdictions. The sheer size difference between the parties, the awakening of the victim to see the defendant on top of her, and the lack of communication could, taken together, constitute a key element of the crime, the use of force. *Mack v. State*, 792 S.E.2d 120 (Ga. App. 2016).

131. **Answer A is the best answer.** Under the common law, and still in most states, rape requires the use of physical force or threat of force resulting in serious bodily harm to compel the victim to have sex. Va. Code § 18.2-61. Courts and legislatures still generally find that threats other than those likely to result in serious bodily harm are insufficient for the crime. The threat of losing a job, a contract, or a scholarship would be insufficient to show force or lack of consent. Although the government would argue that Paola was compelled by Bill's threat, most, though not all, courts would find his actions to fall outside the statutory prohibition. *Murphy v. Commonwealth*, 509 S.W.3d 34 (Ky. 2017). For this reason, **answer C is wrong.** While rape is viewed as a violent crime, the threatened use of actual force would be a sufficient basis for the successful prosecution of the offense even without an expression of protest, as noted above. Hence, **answer B is not the best answer. Answer D is wrong** because Paola seemed not to consent. The problem here is not one of consent, but rather no showing of use of force.

132. **Answer B is the best answer.** The traditional approach to "statutory rape" was that sex with a child under the age of consent (set by law) was rape, regardless of whether the child had consented or not. The view was that the minor could not make an informed decision, and therefore could not consent to sex. The modern approach in some states now permits a defense of reasonable mistake in the context of "statutory rape" in which the child is near the age of consent. Ind. Code § 35-42.4-3. The likelihood that such a defense will be successful, however, depends largely upon the child's age. The younger the child, the less likely courts will accept the defense of reasonable mistake. In such cases, the offense approaches strict liability on this matter. In these circumstances, Brandon had good reason to believe that Cate was an adult so that he may be able to rely upon a defense of reasonable mistake to the crime of rape. *Pelayo-Garcia v. Holder*, 589 F.3d 1010 (9th Cir. 2009).

Cate did seemingly agree to the sexual intercourse. When a child is under the statutorily defined age of consent, the law makes a presumption that the girl could not make an informed decision and could not legally consent to sex. Thus, absent a defense of reasonable mistake, consent of a minor to the sex act is irrelevant. For example, if Cate had been 12 instead of 17, a court would probably not accept such a defense from Brandon and whether or not Cate consented to the sex would be irrelevant for a statutory rape charge. Because the important inquiry raised by this question is whether a court would allow a defense of reasonable mistake, not whether Cate consented to the sex act, **answer A is incorrect.**

Cate is under the age of consent. Legally, she is presumed to be incapable of consenting to sex. At common law, Brandon would have been guilty of rape; the age of consent was a "bright line" limit under which a child could not consent to sex. As the modern approach would allow Brandon the defense of a reasonable mistake, he might not be guilty of rape in jurisdictions following this approach. Because **answer C** restates the common law rule and does not take into account recent modifications to that approach, **answer C is not the best answer. Answer D is also not correct,** for Brandon had the requisite state of mind, but may still be found not guilty of the crime of statutory rape. Rape is unusual in that the *mens rea* for the defendant is, for all practical purposes, merely the intent to have sexual intercourse (not the intent to commit rape). Here Brandon intended to have sexual intercourse. However, given the extenuating circumstances (Brandon's reasonable belief that Cate was "of age" and that sex with her was legal), he may have a defense of reasonable mistake.

133. **The best answer is answer C.** While at common law husbands, as a matter of law, could not be found guilty of raping their wives, all jurisdictions today reject that broad ban. Neb. Rev. Stat. § 28-319. Hence, **answer A is wrong** today. Threatening the victim and throwing her onto the bed and then having intercourse with her could certainly be sufficient evidence to demonstrate the use of force for the purpose of the crime of rape, so **answer B is not correct. Answer D also is not correct** as the marital status may be relevant to the prosecution. That is, while the broad ban on marital rape has been eliminated, some states do look to the marital relationship as being of significance in determining if a crime has been committed. In some states, there is only a crime if the parties are living apart, while in other states there is a specific time for reporting sexual assaults by marital partners. S.C. Code Ann. §§ 16–3–658, 615.

134. **It depends.** For most of our history, the crime of rape was viewed as being committed by a male against a female. Under a traditional common law view of the crime of rape, a man could not be found guilty of raping another man. Even today, some jurisdictions have rape statutes that are gender specific, limited to sexual assaults by men against women. Ga. Code Ann. § 16-6-1. Increasingly, however, such statutes are gender neutral so that a man could be found guilty of raping another man. Typically, these statutes describe various kinds of sexual assaults, not simply those involving vaginal entry, and speak in terms of *persons* being victims and being perpetrators. N.D.C.C. § 12.1–20–02.

135. The fornication crime, dating back hundreds of years, makes sexual intercourse between unmarried people illegal. Under the traditional common law view, then, **answer C would be correct.** It is the wrong answer, however, because most jurisdictions today have either repealed or overturned such laws. **Answer B, therefore, is the best answer.**

      Answer A is not the correct answer, as there is no clear, definitive ruling by the United States Supreme Court that fornication laws are unconstitutional, though several courts have so held. **Answer D is wrong,** as the search here was conducted pursuant to a valid warrant. As a result, there would not be any constitutional violation from the search as indicated by the facts.

136. **Answer C is the best answer.** In *Lawrence v. Texas*, 539 U.S. 558 (2003) the Supreme Court held that with regard to intimate sexual behavior, "liberty protects the person from unwarranted government intrusions into a dwelling or other private places." For that reason, **answer B is clearly incorrect. Answer A is also not correct,** for there is no legal distinction between evidence at trial which is direct and evidence which is circumstantial. **Answer D is wrong** because the language in the statute is sufficiently clear as to withstand constitutional scrutiny.

Causation

137. **Answer C is the best answer.** For a conviction of involuntary manslaughter, there must be a causal relationship between the illegal act and the death. *Commonwealth v. McCloskey*, 835 A.2d 801 (Pa. Super. Ct. 2003). Douglas did not drown as a result of boating or waterskiing in a location where those activities were illegal. Douglas fell into the water and drowned as a result of his intoxication. If Douglas had been boating in another area, he would still have drowned, so his proximity to the rocky outcroppings was unrelated to his drowning. Therefore, the violation is not a "but for" cause of the drowning.

Answer A is not correct because violating the rule against boating or waterskiing near the rocks was not the cause of Douglas's death. Robert would be responsible if the drowning had occurred while Douglas skied and Robert, while operating the boat, steered in a manner that caused Douglas to crash into a rocky outcropping. In that case, Robert would be liable because he was in control of the boat and had insisted on boating and skiing in an unsafe location. For that reason, **answer B is also not the best answer.** Douglas is responsible for his own actions, including drinking excessively while on the lake. **Answer D is not right** because the tort defense of contributory negligence does not exist in the criminal law. Under some circumstances a person may be criminally liable for the knowing, but foolish, actions of another. *State v. Pierce*, 718 S.E.2d 648 (N.C. App. 2011).

138. **Answer C is the best answer.** A person is held responsible for an intervening cause of death only if that cause is foreseeable. Although leaving Trinity alone in the wilderness may have put her at risk, a reasonable person would not expect it to result in this type of death or serious bodily injury. It was not foreseeable that a branch would snap off and land on Trinity. Megan had no reason to expect that a branch would fall at that time and in that place, so Trinity's death was not foreseeable. **Answer A is not the right answer** because involuntary manslaughter requires more than simply negligent behavior. To be guilty of involuntary manslaughter, Megan's actions must be reckless, seriously endangering the safety of another person. Recklessness is behavior that shows a conscious and blatant disregard for human life. Reckless behavior may cause serious injury or even death. **Answer B is not correct** because Megan's wandering off in the woods, leaving Trinity to hike alone for a short time, would not normally result in serious bodily injury or death. If Megan had abandoned Trinity in the North Woods without proper attire or food or transportation, she could be guilty of involuntary manslaughter because serious injury or death would be foreseeable. Under those circumstances, it might be foreseeable that Trinity would become ill as a result of exposure, catch hypothermia and die, or that she would encounter a hungry wild animal and fall victim to an attack. In that situation, Megan's acts would be reckless and she could have reasonably foreseen Trinity's demise. **Answer D is wrong** because Megan did not have to intend to harm Trinity to be guilty of involuntary manslaughter. Intent to harm is not an element of involuntary manslaughter.

139. **Yes,** Megan may well be convicted on the manslaughter charge now. While death from a falling tree limb may not be very likely, death from a heart attack is quite foreseeable in a situation in which Megan knew that Trinity would be terribly afraid. Abandoning someone in the wilderness who is afraid of such a setting and might suffer ill effects caused by her heightened state of fear is truly reckless behavior likely to result in some sort of serious injury. The key issue is foreseeability, and that issue is resolved on a case by case basis, being quite fact specific. *State v. Fisher*, 745 S.E.2d 894 (N.C. App. 2013).

140. **Answer A is the best answer.** While Flo's own action directly contributed to her death, it was the brutal beating by Jessie that caused Flo to be in the hospital and to receive the message as to her permanent disfigurement. Under these extreme circumstances, though the death may not have been intended by Jessie, it was foreseeable. *Brackett v. Peters*, 11 F.3d 78 (7th Cir. 1993). **Answer B is wrong** because foreseeability is required for criminal responsibility with such an intervening event.

   While Flo's action in pulling out the tube in fact caused her death, in the situation described above, such action by the victim does not relieve the defendant of criminal responsibility. The death is still deemed foreseeable. Hence, **answer C is not correct.** For the same reason, **answer D is also not correct.** Even intervening negligence in such a situation will not break the chain of causation. The defendant is criminally responsible because her brutal behavior created an extremely high-risk situation. *Brackett v. Peters, supra.*

141. **Answer B is correct.** An individual's reckless behavior must be the proximate cause—both the but-for cause and legal cause—of a victim's death in order to support a conviction for involuntary manslaughter. *Beckwitt v. State*, 245 A.3d 201 (Md. Spec. App. 2021). But for Eric hiring Jeremy to dig tunnels in a dangerous environment, Jeremy would not have died. **Answer A is not the best answer**, because while restricting access to the main floor played a role is fostering a dangerous work environment, it was not the proximate cause of Jeremy's death. **Answer C is not correct**, because Eric did not have to intentionally start the fire in order for his actions to be grossly reckless or inherently dangerous. And for legal causation, the resulting harm need not be actually foreseen, only that a reasonable person would foresee the harm as being reasonably related to Eric's actions. Therefore, **answer D is not correct.**

Defenses

SELF-DEFENSE

142.   **Answer C is the best answer.** Under the general rule of self-defense, a person can use whatever non-lethal force appears to be reasonably necessary to prevent immediate harm to herself. An individual can use deadly force in self-defense in more limited situations. However, a killing committed by a defendant in self-defense is justified under the law if she reasonably believed that: (1) she was in imminent danger at the time she took an action; and (2) deadly force was necessary in response to the perceived danger. *Littler v. State*, 871 N.E.2d 276 (Ind. 2007). Under the circumstances, Maggie could have reasonably believed that she was in imminent danger of serious bodily injury and that she swung the baseball bat because it was necessary to respond to the threat posed. Thus, she can argue that her actions should be protected as made in self-defense. The jury should receive an instruction on self-defense in this case. **Answer A is not the right answer** because an endangered person does not have to wait until an aggressor has already acted in any specific aggressive manner before the person is entitled to defend herself. So long as Maggie reasonably believed both that she was in imminent danger at the time she hit the man and that the potentially deadly force was necessary in response to this danger, the jury should be able to consider whether Maggie's actions should be deemed self-defense. With the facts presented, it is not clear that Maggie could have safely escaped in her car. Under the law, a person only has a duty to retreat before using deadly force in one's own defense if it is clear that such an escape can be made without incurring bodily harm. Therefore, **answer B is incorrect. Answer D is also incorrect.** Maggie's subjective belief that she was in imminent danger would not be sufficient for her actions to be deemed self-defense. In presenting a self-defense claim, the defendant's belief is based principally upon an objective, rather than a subjective, standard. In order to get the benefit of this defense, a reasonable person in her circumstances must have believed that she was in imminent danger and that her actions were necessary to respond to this apparent danger.

143.   For the self-defense assertion to succeed, the belief that the use of force is necessary and that the amount of force used is necessary only has to be reasonable. It does not have to be correct in fact. Mistake is permitted. For this reason, the stranger's actual intentions do not affect the outcome. Therefore, if Maggie was justified in using potentially deadly force against the man, the fact that she was not actually in danger does not change the result, the standard is linked to a reasonable — not necessarily accurate — belief. *Cruz-West v. Superintendent*, 2020 WL 1036082 (E.D. Pa. 2020).

144.   **Answer B is the best answer.** In order to respond to another person with deadly force, one must reasonably believe that he is faced with imminent danger of serious bodily injury or death and that deadly force is necessary to respond to the threat posed. Under these facts, the parking lot stranger was faced with a threat, but not with serious bodily injury or death. Given their relative sizes and the use of a hurled cell phone as opposed to the usual sort of deadly weapon, a reasonable person would have seen that he could have disarmed Maggie or otherwise avoided killing her. *State v. Qualls*, 439 P.3d 301 (Kan. 2019). Because a person is generally not entitled to rely upon self-defense in using deadly force if he could reasonably and safely have avoided using deadly force, the stranger could not rely upon such a defense under these facts. **Answer A is not correct** because deadly force may sometimes be used in self-defense. Normally, deadly force can only be used to prevent apparent serious bodily injury or death, from which the person could not safely escape. Given the circumstances in this scenario, however, the stranger could not rely upon the defense of self in his use of deadly force. **Answer D is not the right answer** because the stranger's subjective beliefs are not sufficient to warrant the use of deadly force. In order to rely upon the defense of self-defense, the stranger's belief in the apparent imminent danger and his belief that the amount of force he used was necessary both must be objectively reasonable. **Answer C is also wrong.** Even if Maggie threw the phone with such force so as to make it a dangerous weapon, other factors such as the relative size of the parties and other weapons must be considered in determining the nature of the threat posed and the ability of the person threatened to safely escape. Additional factors that may be relevant in this consideration are the age and health of the parties, the presence of multiple assailants, or a past history of violence between the parties. *Evenson v. State*, 177 P.3d 819 (Wyo. 2008).

145.   **Answer A is the best answer.** There is no constitutional requirement that with affirmative defenses the burden be on one party or another. That is a matter of policy for the state, as held by the Supreme Court in *Dixon v. United States*, 548 U.S. 1 (2006). **Answer C is therefore clearly not correct. Answer B is not the best answer** because this defense is not limited to homicide cases. **Answer D is not right** because it confuses two fundamental concepts. The government in a criminal case must always prove the elements of the crime beyond a reasonable doubt. For defenses, however, there is no comparable due process requirement as to the standard of proof.

146.   **Answer C is the best answer.** Since Carl was the aggressor, Lenny would have a right to use force in response if such force would be necessary to prevent further bodily harm. If a person generally could retreat from a violent situation without experiencing physical harm, then the use of force is not necessary, and the person cannot rely upon an argument of self-defense in some states. Lenny could have retreated (either before or after Carl's shove) without resorting to violence. The exception to this retreat rule, however,

is when the altercation occurs in the defendant's home. W. Va. Code § 55-7-22. For this reason, **answer B is not the best answer. Answer A is also not the best answer.** An act need not be extremely violent in order to make a person an aggressor. Carl's shove, which appeared designed to provoke a physical confrontation, was more than enough to make Carl the aggressor. **Answer D is incorrect.** The law does not permit unrestricted "tit-for-tat" behaviors. Although one may act in self-defense when he reasonably believes that force is necessary to avoid bodily harm, the law does not protect a person who has used force when an alternative to the use of force was available. The fact that a person has been attacked does not necessarily protect his response as self-defense.

147. **Yes.** Under modern "stand your ground" statutes, the defendant may not need to retreat in public. This is the case even if the defendant could easily and safely retreat without using force to defend himself. *See, e.g.,* Ohio Revised Code § 2901.09.

148. **Answer A is the best answer.** Although resistance to unlawful arrests was once considered acceptable, more than half of the states have now made it illegal to resist an arrest, whether lawful or unlawful. *State v. Mann*, 237 P.3d 966 (Wash. App. 2010). Underlying this trend is the notion that violence, particularly against peace officers, is not the best way to resolve conflicts and that citizens should rely on the modern criminal justice system to protect their rights. Thus, **answer C is incorrect. Answer B is not right** because it does not comport with the facts described. In these circumstances, the officers initiated the conflict when they confronted Tien. Thus, if the two individuals were not police officers, Tien could perhaps have relied upon self-defense as a justification for her actions. This conflict, however, arose from an attempted arrest by police officers. **Answer D is not the best answer** because it fails to take into account the fact that the individuals Tien encountered were police officers who were trying to question and then arrest her. Of course, the fact that Tien was outnumbered would normally be relevant to a claim of self-defense (e.g., to examine whether Tien could have reasonably retreated from the situation and the extent of the threat posed).

149. **Perhaps.** If Tien genuinely and reasonably believed these two people were not police officers, she would then be able to claim self-defense as a defense to her actions. This result would depend on several factors such as what the officers said and whether they first showed Tien identification.

150. **Answer B is the best answer.** The person who starts a fight by acting as the aggressor cannot claim self-defense. In addition, a person is barred from the justification of self-defense if he escalates the amount of force being used. In this scenario, Jared began a shoving match. Sanjay's use of a knife increased the amount of harm that was likely to result from the altercation. Thus, he escalated the conflict and as such Sanjay is barred from a claim of self-defense. *State v. Marks*, 602 P.2d 1344 (Kan. 1979). **Answer A is therefore incorrect.** Although Jared started the fight, Sanjay became the aggressor when he pulled a knife. A defendant may only use a lawful amount of force in self-defense.

Such a lawful amount of force is that level of force that reasonably appears necessary to prevent harm to one's person. Any force beyond that level is deemed unlawful force. In using unlawful force, a person (even a person who was initially a victim) becomes the aggressor. In this case, Sanjay's use of the knife was an unlawful response to Jared's shove because that level of force was not required to avoid the harm Jared might have caused. As a result, **answer C is wrong.** In a fight between two individuals, in which neither is using a weapon, the introduction of a deadly weapon generally constitutes an unlawful escalation. Although the knife in this case did not cause any serious injuries to Jared, Sanjay's use of the knife was unlawful. Sanjay's unlawful use of force transformed him into the fight's aggressor. As such, he was unable to claim self-defense, regardless of how much harm he actually caused with the knife. Because the actual level of harm caused to Jared is irrelevant to whether Sanjay can claim self-defense, **answer D is not correct.**

151. **Answer C is the best answer.** Lola had a great deal of evidence demonstrating that she had been the victim of an abusive spouse for many years. Battered victims may be able to predict violent outbursts more accurately than a casual observer. Therefore, Lola knew that Mel was going to become extremely violent the night he died, even though he had not yet made any threats against Lola. Most states now allow evidence of battered victim syndrome in circumstances in which the battered victim suffers from an inability to remove him/herself from an abusive relationship. Ky. Rev. Stat. Ann. § 503.050. The syndrome has been used in the self-defense context to show that a battered victim may act before the abusive person's actions become life-threatening. *State v. Elzey*, 244 A.3d 1068 (Md. 2021). The battered victim syndrome may be seen as a relaxation of the traditional requirement, for a claim of self-defense, that the harm defended against must be imminent. Therefore, **answer B is not the best answer.** One is almost never required to retreat from one's own home. Although the issue is more complicated when the assailant lives in the same place as the victim, most states would not require Lola to leave her home. In addition, because Lola may be able to present a self-defense claim relying upon battered victim syndrome, **answer A is not correct. Answer D is not the best answer** because prior incidents do not automatically justify the use of deadly force. Prior violent behavior may, however, be used to show the reasonableness of a defendant's fear of serious bodily injury. Particularly in the case of battered victim syndrome, courts often allow the use of deadly force after prior violent behavior with the expectation that violent behavior will occur again immediately.

152. **D is the best answer.** The aggressor of violence is not entitled to self-defense unless she withdraws completely from the physical struggle. Such withdrawal requires an abandonment of violence perceived by the other party, and a simple retreat from the fight will not constitute a withdrawal. *State v. Pride*, 567 S.W.2d 426 (Mo. 1978). Here, Jane began the chain of violence by punching Mike. **Answer B is wrong** because, when Barry intervened to stop Jane, the violence was still ongoing so Jane cannot claim withdrawal. Jane did run away at the end, but that was after she had already punched Barry. As such, Jane, the aggressor, cannot claim self-defense. **Answer C is wrong** because, although

Mike did start the altercation, he committed no violence or criminal act that would render him the aggressor. **Answer A is wrong** because Jane is still the aggressor, although the subjective elements of the self-defense claims may have been satisfied.

153. **Answer C is the best answer.** In most jurisdictions, using force to defend others is justified if one reasonably believes that she is acting to prevent an unlawful assault. Under this rule, the party intervening to stop the violence only has to act upon reasonable belief. Here, Janette saw Minho raise his fist against Danny in a dimly lit and unpopulated parking lot, which gave rise to a reasonable belief that Minho was assaulting Danny. **Answer B is wrong** because it follows the logic of the historical common law rule, which stated that one may intervene to defend another if the defended person could engage in an act of self-defense. Under this *alter ego* approach, Janette would not have been allowed to intervene because Danny, who was only practicing his play, would not have been allowed to use violence to defend himself. **Answer A is wrong** because one may act to rescue another despite the lack of a special relationship, and **answer D is wrong** because the law in most cases does not place an absolute duty to act in aid of others.

DEFENSE OF OTHERS

154. **Answer C is the best answer.** Richard could attack the man if Richard used a necessary amount of force based upon a reasonable belief that the man posed a serious threat to the child. The approach used in most states today allows defenders to use reasonable force to defend someone whom they reasonably believe is being unlawfully attacked. In this case, Richard need only reasonably believe that force is necessary to protect the child in order to rely upon a claim of defense of others. *Smith v. State*, 480 P;3d 532 (Wyo. 2021). **Answer A is not right** because it reflects the approach embodied in an old rule that is no longer used in most states. The old rule restricted the use of force in defense of others to those with whom the defender had a special relationship (e.g., parent and child, employer and employee). Unlike that old approach, the modern, majority view encourages strangers and friends to assist one another when they are threatened with harm.

  Answer B is not correct because bystanders are not required to wait and gather all of the facts before assisting someone who appears to be in immediate danger of bodily harm. Instead, one may act on behalf of another so long as he has a reasonable belief that the person being assisted is in immediate danger of unlawful, bodily harm. **Answer D is wrong** because it reflects an approach no longer incorporated into most modern statutes. The older rule, known as the "alter ego" view, discouraged strangers from interfering with one another by punishing those who acted based upon a misunderstanding of the situation. Under the old law, Richard would only be justified to act on the child's behalf if the child would be permitted to use the same amount of force in self-defense. The test today, however, is whether the individual acted reasonably under the circumstances.

155. **Answer A is the best answer.** Richard acted based on a reasonable belief that the man posed a serious threat to the child. Under the modern, majority view, mistakes are permitted. This approach encourages people to come to the aid of others by not punishing those who act out of an intent to help someone in need, even if all of the facts relating to the situation are not uncovered before action is taken. The result would be the same whether the man was actually trying to abduct the child or whether he was trying to prevent the abduction of his child, so long as it reasonably appeared to be an abduction. Texas Penal Code, Title 2, § 9.33. Therefore, **answer C is wrong. Answer B is incorrect** because Richard was justified in acting, under the modern approach, in both sets of circumstances. Under the old approach, this answer would be correct because Richard did not have a special, protected relationship with the child. **Answer D is not the best answer** because the child's justification is not relevant to the question asked. As noted above, the old approach to defense of others (also known as the "alter ego" rule) is no longer used in most states.

156. Under the historical, "common law" rule discussed above, the pedestrian's actions would not be justified. Using this "alter ego" rule, the pedestrian would only be justified to act in defense of Wilfredo if Wilfredo would have been permitted to use the same amount of force in self-defense. Wilfredo would not be allowed to resist the arrest by the security guard, because the arrest, in response to Wilfredo's shoplifting, was lawful. Therefore, the pedestrian would not be justified in defending Wilfredo. *State v. Mayo,* 113 A.3d 250 (N.H. 2015). This is the main argument in favor of the "alter ego" rule; it protects individuals from well-meaning, but misguided, members of the public. With the modern, majority rule, the pedestrian's actions would be permitted. This approach allows one to act on behalf of another if he reasonably believes that the amount of force is necessary to prevent bodily harm. The pedestrian saw Wilfredo being attacked by another man and reasonably thought that force was necessary to stop this apparent attack. Although the pedestrian was mistaken about the situation, he was justified in using force to prevent further bodily harm to Wilfredo. The modern approach encourages bystanders to act on behalf of others and allows mistakes, so long as a reasonable person would have acted as the defender did.

DEFENSE OF PROPERTY

157. **Answer B is the best answer.** Deadly force at common law was not justified to protect personal property. A reasonable amount of force may be used to prevent the theft of property. However, the law provides that deadly force used simply to stop the theft of property is not reasonable. *People v. Zinda,* 183 Cal. Rptr. 3d 558 (Cal. App. 2015). Almost any other type of force, short of deadly force, used to prevent the theft of property might be reasonable. As human life is valued higher than any amount of property, including a fancy car, **answer D is not right. Answer A is the wrong answer.** As explained above, the use of deadly force is not a reasonable amount of force to use in defense of property. The use of a firearm is considered deadly force, even in circumstances in which the person targeted does not die. Although **answer C contains a correct statement of the law**, this statement is incomplete. The use of force is permitted to prevent or stop the imminent theft of property, provided that the amount of force is reasonable. Because the use of deadly force to protect personal property alone is not reasonable, **answer C is incorrect.**

158. **Perhaps,** as several jurisdictions have laws which specifically indicate that one "may use deadly force upon another when and to the extent the person reasonably believes it is necessary to terminate what the person reasonably believes to be a carjacking of that vehicle...." Alaska Stat. § 11.81.350(ex1).

159. **Answer D is the best answer.** Most states provide that one may use deadly force in a home invasion situation if he believes that the criminal is attempting to commit a serious crime, such force is necessary to prevent the offense, and the use of non-deadly force to prevent the crime would expose the defendant or another innocent person to substantial risk of serious bodily injury. New York Penal Law § 35.20. Seeing the burglar at the foot of the stairs, Santiago could reasonably have thought that the man was a danger. As a result, Santiago could have believed that force was necessary to stop the man, and that the use of non-deadly force would have put Santiago or his family at great risk. Most states allow the use of deadly force to prevent crimes in one's home. Under this approach, one does not have to permit a thief to take violent action in order to avoid a killing. For this reason, **answer A is not the best answer. Answer B is not the correct answer.** Santiago did not have to attempt non-deadly means to stop the man if Santiago believed reasonably that to do so would endanger his family. If Santiago thought that the use of non-deadly force would endanger him or his family, he was not under an obligation to use such force as an alternative to deadly force. **Answer C is wrong** because it is too general. The laws in many, but not all, states do not permit one to use deadly force whenever a dwelling is burglarized. However, generally a defendant must actually believe that the use of such force is necessary to prevent a more serious crime, or a physical harm to himself or to another innocent person before the use of deadly force can be justified.

160. Santiago's argument would likely be more forceful in a jurisdiction with a "stand your ground" statute. These laws, adopted in a number of states, often have a presumption of danger from the mere presence of an intruder in the home. "A person is presumed to have held a reasonable fear of imminent peril of death or great bodily harm to himself or herself or another when using or threatening to use defensive force that is intended or likely to cause death or great bodily harm to another" if: "...The person against whom the defensive force was used or threatened was in the process of unlawfully and forcefully entering, or had unlawfully and forcibly entered, a dwelling, residence, or occupied vehicle...." Fla. Stat. § 776.013.

DURESS

161. **Yes.** The elements of the common law defense of duress are: (1) another person threatens serious bodily harm or death to the defendant or a third person; (2) the defendant reasonably believes that the threat is real; (3) the threat is imminent at the time the crime is committed; (4) no reasonable escape exists; and (5) the defendant is blameless for the instigation of the threat. *United States v. Haischer*, 780 F.3d 1277 (9th Cir. 2015). The statutory defense of duress is generally similar to the common law defense of duress, but may vary somewhat, from one jurisdiction to another, in the application of each element. In order for Casey to rely upon the defense of duress, all of the elements of the defense must be satisfied for each of the crimes with which he is charged. Casey may properly assert the defense of duress for the traffic violations he committed. Casey assumed that the man pointing the gun at him posed a serious physical threat to Casey. In this case, Casey reasonably believed that the threat of serious bodily harm was real and that the threat was imminent. Although Casey might have been able to escape from the car, there was also the real chance he could have been killed. Under the law, Casey acted appropriately when compliance with the stranger's requests could have preserved his life. Finally, Casey did not do anything to provoke or create the threat of the gunman.

162. The defense of duress for the killing of the friend will fail. Duress is not a defense to a purposeful killing. *Commonwealth v. Vasquez*, 971 N.E.2d 783 (Mass. 2012). In some states in which duress has been codified, duress may be used as a mitigating factor to reduce the penalty for a murder or even to drop the crime charged from murder to manslaughter. Nonetheless, duress in such circumstances is not a full defense.

163. **Answer B is the best answer.** Under the law, threats of economic reprisals, property damage, damage to one's reputation, and even minor injuries do not justify committing a criminal act. *State v. Lopez-Navor*, 951 A.3d 508 (R.I. 2008). A person may only claim duress when a threat of serious bodily injury or death has been made against him or a third person. Raul was threatened with the loss of his job — an economic hardship — so he may not use the defense of duress.

One of the elements of a defense of duress is that the threat must be imminent. If Daphne's threat were imminent, that fact would weigh in *favor* of Raul's ability to use the defense. **Answer A is incorrect** both because the crime did not involve threats of deadly force or great bodily harm and because it is a misstatement of an element of duress. Here, Daphne probably could not have immediately implemented her threat. Raul would have had time to consult with Daphne's superiors, an attorney, or law enforcement officers. This answer would be correct if it began "No, as the threat was NOT imminent."

Because Daphne was his boss, Raul reasonably believed that her threat was genuine. The reasonable belief of the person being threatened that the threat is real and credible is only one of the elements of duress. **Answer C is not the best answer** because the other elements of the defense (such as imminence and threat of deadly force) are not satisfied. Although one element of the defense of duress is that the person did not create or contribute to the creation of the coercive situation (which would be satisfied in this case because Raul did not provoke Daphne's actions), **answer D is not the right answer** because the other elements of the defense of duress are not satisfied. For example, one may not use the defense of duress if there is a reasonable escape from the threat other than to comply with the demands. Raul could have spoken to Daphne's superiors, probably kept his job, and not complied with her demands. In addition, as explained above, the nature of the threat would not warrant a defense of duress.

164. **The best answer is D.** While the defense of duress is available to defendants who commit crimes under imminent and immediate harm such as the ones that Peter faced in this example, it does not protect actors who recklessly insert themselves into situations where they would be put under duress. *Williams v. State*, 646 A.2d. 1101 (Md. Ct. Spec. App. 1994). Here, Peter voluntarily bought drugs from Mary, a known blackmailer, making it likely that he would be put under duress by her. **Answers A and B** are proper elements of the duress defense; the defense can be successful if the harm to the defendant was imminent and the defendant could not have escaped from the harm. However, Peter cannot successfully claim duress despite satisfying these elements, because he was acting recklessly. **Answer C is incorrect** because Peter was reckless, and he could not have been concerned about the safety of nephews whom Mary could not immediately reach.

NECESSITY

165. **Answer C is the best answer.** The defense of necessity allows one to violate laws for reasons of social policy. When obeying the law would result in greater harm than that created by the violation of the laws, one may claim the defense of necessity. *State v. St. Cyr*, 2021 WL 4891065 (Ia. App. 2021). The bodily injury that would have resulted from obeying the laws against trespass, theft, etc. far outweighs the harm created when Malik used the shelter and supplies. A person may not use the defense of necessity when he has created the problematic situation. Because Malik had no reason to expect a winter storm, his lack of preparation did not cause his predicament. Therefore, **answer A is not the best answer.**

Answer B is wrong because the defense of necessity may be used whenever there is the possibility that a violation of the law will result in a lesser harm than if the law is obeyed. Necessity is not limited to life and death situations. The defense of necessity exists to achieve a just result. Most cases of necessity involve a serious harm that would result from obeying the law, but such a result need not rise to the level of involving a choice between life and death. Malik may claim necessity when the predicament he faced involved a choice between bodily injury and harm to property. In virtually all cases, the interest in human health and safety will outweigh property concerns in a determination of whether individuals can rely upon the defense of necessity. **Answer D is not the**

right answer because it is too extreme. A person faced with a situation involving a choice between preserving human safety and a property interest may almost always choose human health and safety and the law will protect that choice by enabling the person to rely upon the defense of necessity. However, a person cannot do anything and everything necessary to preserve one's own life. For example, a person cannot choose to cause serious bodily harm or death to another in order to preserve one's own life.

166. **Malik would not have a good defense.** As with duress, the defense here would not be available to one who was to blame for creating the underlying problem. *State v. Healy*, 237 P.3d 360 (Wash. App. 2010). Proof that Malik ignored warnings and did not prepare properly might well defeat his claim.

167. **Answer A is the best answer.** Financial necessity is generally not a defense to any crime. Necessity is a defense based on social policy. The violation of a law is presumed to result in a greater harm than any harm that could be created by economic hardship. In addition, most instances of economic hardship will have some sort of legal remedy. One may not claim necessity when there is a way to lawfully avoid the harm. *United States v. Al-Rekabi*, 454 F.3d 1113 (10th Cir. 2006). **Answer B is incorrect** and is a red herring. Regardless of whether Immanuel was charged in a state following the common law or a modern statute, he could not rely upon the defense of necessity for forging a check to pay a mortgage payment because of dire financial circumstances.

Although necessity is a defense based on social policy, it is designed to prevent injustice resulting from the application of the law. One may not use the defense of necessity in a situation where the legislature has already weighed the harms and decided against the criminal act. Foreclosure is a recognized financial tool. Although legislators may indicate a preference for home ownership through other legislation, the law also clearly indicates that foreclosure is an acceptable remedy for the failure to make mortgage payments. The societal harm caused by fraud outweighs Immanuel's personal gain from sending a forged check. For this reason, **answer C is not the best answer.** Whether Immanuel was able to pay the bill a week, a month, or even a day later, does not address the balancing of "evils" that the necessity defense requires. The defense of necessity is permitted when the harm resulting from obeying the law would cause a greater harm than breaking the law. Fraud disrupts many societal institutions. Immanuel's short-term personal gain does not outweigh the social harm created by fraud. Immanuel's efforts to lessen the harm of his actions do not excuse him, so **answer D is not correct.**

168. **Answer B is the best answer.** One is not excused from criminal acts on the basis of necessity when a lawful option is available. *Commonwealth v. Craig*, 2021 WL 4739495 (Pa. Super. 2021). Although speaking to the prison officials might not have been helpful, Dennis could have written to the head of the department of corrections, to legislators, or even to the press. In addition, Dennis could have raised his claims in the judicial system by filing a legal action. Because Dennis could have pursued these legal options, he

cannot rely upon necessity as a defense to the criminal acts. **Answer A is not the right answer.** The United States Supreme Court has indicated, in *United States v. Bailey*, 444 U.S. 394 (1980), that a prisoner may be excused from escaping from prison if certain criteria are met. State courts have also decided that prisoners do not have to accept egregious treatment. The inmates, though, must show that the avoided harm is very extreme and clearly imminent, such as one escaping from a beating or a prison fire. As indicated above, prisoners facing less imminent and egregious harms have other avenues to pursue. Although states have taken a variety of approaches, they generally agree that a prisoner may escape out of necessity if the prison is on fire or she is directly threatened. Although a prisoner has a right to preserve her own life, the circumstances in which courts have allowed a defense of necessity for escape are extremely narrow. Dennis was not in such a desperate situation. In addition, all of the other elements of the defense of necessity were not met. Therefore, **answer C is not correct.** In order to be excused for the escape from a prison, the escapee must show that there was no legal alternative, that the harm avoided was severe enough to warrant the violation of a sentence of imprisonment (in most cases, serious bodily injury or death), and that the danger avoided was imminent. In this case, Dennis had been enduring the prison's abhorrent conditions for two years, and could likely have continued living under such conditions for several more years. While the conditions were despicable, Dennis apparently faced no immediate danger. Dennis would not be excused for escaping from the prison because the harm was not imminent and was not sufficiently serious. Therefore, **answer D is wrong.**

169.   **Answer C is the best answer.** For the necessity defense to hold, the alleged harm avoided must be imminent and not distant. *State v. Warshow*, 410 A.2d 1000 (Vt. 1979). In this case, it was arguably uncertain that Anne would have caught the virus from being in proximity with Tom, even if the virus was contagious. The necessity defense is available when obeying the law would result in harm greater than the harm from violating the law. In this case, however, Anne would have difficulty arguing that the harms caused by her trespass and theft were smaller than the harm she avoided, as the virus that year was not particularly deadly despite being highly contagious. As such, **answer B is not correct. Answer A is wrong** because Anne could have simply turned around and walked back the way she came to avoid being in proximity with Tom. **Answer D is wrong** because, even if she arguably put herself in a situation with a high likelihood of exposure to unmasked people, going into her dorm building was not a reckless behavior on Anne's part.

PREVENTION OF CRIME

170.   **Answer B is the best answer.** In *Tennessee v. Garner*, 471 U.S. 1 (1985), the Supreme Court held that an officer may only use deadly force when she has "probable cause to believe that the suspect poses a threat of serious physical harm, either to the officer or

to others." Because Mike was fleeing and did not appear armed, and because the officer had no reason to think that Mike had committed or would commit "a crime involving the infliction or threatened infliction of serious physical harm," the officer was not entitled under the law to use deadly force. Therefore, the officer may not rely upon the defense of crime prevention or law enforcement for the use of deadly force. Under the common law, police officers had a great deal more discretion to use deadly force to stop crimes or effectuate arrests. However, in *Garner*, the Court imposed a constitutional limit on the police power to use deadly force. A police officer may use deadly force to effectuate an arrest of a fleeing felon only if the officer has probable cause to believe that the suspect poses a threat of serious bodily harm to the officers or others. **Answer A is not the right answer** as there are times when deadly force is appropriate. **Answer C is not correct** because it predicates the use of deadly force on the commission of a serious crime rather than on the danger Mike posed to the officer or others. *Garner* prohibits an officer from using deadly force unless the felon poses an apparent danger of serious bodily harm either to the officer or to innocent bystanders. Therefore, **answer D is wrong**; the officer may not use deadly force in the prevention of crime or to prevent a felon from escaping when the suspect posed no apparent danger of serious bodily harm.

171.   **Yes.** In such a situation, the officer could reasonably believe that it was necessary to shoot Mike as he posed a serious danger to her or to others.

172.   **Answer D is the best answer.** Reasonable force may be used to prevent the commission of crimes. *United States v. Brodhead*, 714 F. Supp. 593 (D. Mass. 1989). Gus could rely upon the defense of crime prevention for the use of force so long as he reasonably believed that the woman was about to commit a crime, and that the use of force was necessary to prevent that crime. **Answer A is not correct.** The standard is reasonable force. Tackling a robbery suspect would not be extreme under the circumstances. **Answer B is also not correct.** Officers may use force either to prevent a crime or to make an arrest. The officer's belief that the force was necessary and that the crime was being (or had been) committed must be reasonable. Moderate force may be used even when there is no danger of bodily harm in order to prevent the commission of a crime. **Answer C is not the best answer** because, at the time he used such force to prevent a crime, Gus did not need to fear for his personal safety.

173.   **Answer C is the best answer.** *Tennessee v. Garner*, 471 U.S. 1 (1985), allows law enforcement officers to use deadly force in the presence of "probable cause to believe . . . threat of serious physical harm." Here, Officer Buddy could reasonably conclude that Ollie posed a serious physical threat because Ollie was holding what appeared to be a handgun given the circumstances. **Answer A is incorrect** because, although *Garner* requires that the law enforcement officer issue a warning if feasible, in this case, the immediacy of the danger posed to Officer Buddy made the warning not feasible. **Answer B is incorrect** because it was objectively reasonable, although erroneous, for Officer Buddy to have concluded that Ollie was holding a handgun as a result of the lights reflected on the

screwdriver. *Harris v. Green*, 2008 WL 5000172 (E.D. Ark. 2008). **Answer D is incorrect** because the prevention of crime defense does not dispositively turn on whether the officer was trying to apprehend a suspect; the officer may use deadly force on a suspect only if there is probable cause to believe that the suspect poses serious harm.

ENTRAPMENT

174. Under the majority subjective test for entrapment, the prosecution must prove beyond a reasonable doubt that the defendant was disposed to commit the crime before an agent first contacted her. *United States v. Jacobson*, 503 U.S. 540 (1992). In spite of Cynthia's earlier conviction, it is clear from her reluctance and the several meetings that she was not inclined to sell drugs when Leon first approached her. **Answer D is the best answer.**

Answer A is incorrect, for if the defendant was predisposed to commit the crime, in most states the defense of entrapment will fail even if the agent provided the drugs. While Cynthia ultimately committed the crime willingly, under the subjective test the important moment for consideration is the time just before the first government contact is made, so **Answer B is wrong.** Under the subjective test, the chief inquiry concerns the defendant's state of mind rather than the nature of the government's inducement. Thus, **Answer C is incorrect.**

175. Cynthia would now be convicted of the offense. With no reluctance, and with the agent simply offering her the opportunity to commit the crime, a decision-maker would likely conclude that Cynthia was predisposed and thus not entrapped. *State v. Mendoza*, 363 P.3d 1231 (N.M.Ct. App. 2015).

176. The objective test for entrapment asks whether a reasonable person would have been induced by the government's behavior to commit the crime. Cynthia may have been more inclined to deal drugs than the average person, but she initially refused to participate in the activities Leon proposed. Cynthia remained hesitant even when faced with dire financial need. She only agreed to deal drugs after Leon had worked very hard to persuade her. Because a reasonable person in Cynthia's position might have been induced to sell drugs based upon Leon's extreme behavior, **answer C is the best answer.** *People v. Barraza*, 591 P.2d 947 (Cal. 1979).

Answer A is not the best answer because Cynthia's eventual agreement to participate in Leon's plan is not relevant to the objective test of entrapment, which focuses on the inducement by the government. The objective test of entrapment examines whether a reasonable person would have agreed to participate in the crime because of the government's actions. The subjective test, adopted in a majority of states, *see* above, examines a defendant's predisposition to commit the crime. Hence, **answer B is wrong** under the objective test because it fails to take into consideration the government's actions, while focusing on the defendant's state of mind. **Answer D is also wrong.** Cynthia dealt drugs before Leon propositioned her. However, she had quit and had indicated to Leon that she did not want to get back into the business. These facts could be taken into account to determine whether Cynthia was predisposed to commit the crime. While such a determination would be relevant in evaluating a claim of entrapment under the subjective test, it would not be as important in evaluating the same claim under the objective test.

177.   **Answer D is the best answer.** The subjective test for entrapment looks primarily to the defendant's predisposition to commit a crime rather than the behavior of the government agent. Although the argument could be made that Alice was likely to commit this crime based upon her prior criminal history, her prostitution offenses occurred years before. Alice appeared to have had no intention of continuing to engage in prostitution. In evaluating the entrapment defense under the subjective test, courts consider whether the defendant would have engaged in the criminal act absent government intervention. *Sherman v. United States*, 356 U.S. 369 (1958). In this case, it is highly unlikely that Alice would have become involved in prostitution at that time absent the undercover policeman's solicitation for such a large amount of money. Therefore, **answer A is not the best answer.**

Although Alice was willing to commit the crime of prostitution in order to make a large amount of money, the decision-maker using the subjective test must examine whether she was otherwise predisposed, prior to being contacted, to engage in prostitution. Therefore, **answer B is not right.** The subjective test considers the culpability of the defendant, whereas the objective test focuses on the government's behavior. The amount of money offered by the police officer would be the crucial factor in an objective test analysis; under the subjective test, however, while the money is relevant, the key question remains: was the defendant predisposed to commit the crime? *United States v. Abreu*, 2021 WL 5123746 (S.D. Miss. 2021). Therefore, **answer C is not correct.**

178.   **Answer A is the best answer.** Under the subjective test for entrapment, the important inquiry is whether the defendant was predisposed to commit the crime. In answering this question, the fact-finder can consider evidence of the defendant's prior crimes in order to show their predisposition to commit the crimes charged. The length of time that has passed since the prior crimes, the type of crimes committed previously, and the willingness of the defendants to commit the current crime are all factors that can be weighed in determining the defendants' states of mind. In this case, the students were drug dealers at the time of Fernando's request and quickly agreed to his proposal. For this reason, the government will be able to prove under the subjective test that they were not entrapped by Fernando.

Under either the objective or the subjective test, a defendant can only be entrapped by a government agent; there is no defense of "private entrapment." Nonetheless, the courts have defined the phrase "government agent" broadly to include citizens working for the government. *Sherman v. United States*, 356 U.S. 369 (1958). Because Fernando was acting on behalf of the government, he would be considered a government agent.

Thus, **answer B is wrong.** Although the police provided the drugs the defendants sold, the subjective test focuses mainly on the culpability of the defendants, not principally the actions of the government. The students were exactly the type of people that the police were trying to catch — known drug dealers. The fact that the police provided the drugs is less important under the subjective test than the predisposition of the students to commit the crime; therefore, **answer C is not the best answer.** *See United States v. Russell*, 411 U.S. 423 (1973). **Answer D is incorrect.** Presumably, no person would commit a crime knowing that she would be caught. The fact that the students would not have sold the drugs had they been aware that Fernando was working for the police does not provide a ground for claiming entrapment. The students cannot show a lack of predisposition to sell drugs simply because they would not have done it in this instance if they had suspected that they would be caught.

179.   **Answer B is the best answer.** The objective test allows people who have committed crimes to go free, even if they are culpable. The threat that culpable people may be released provides an incentive for the police to be careful about the methods used to catch criminals. The objective test assumes that even a law-abiding person can be induced to commit a crime if the reward is substantial enough. The aim of the objective test is to prevent the police from offering such a great incentive for citizens to commit crimes. The subjective test potentially creates different results for the same government behavior based on the defendant's history. For example, the subjective test could preclude a person with a criminal disposition from using the entrapment defense, while allowing a person who had not committed previous crimes to rely on the defense. This result could occur even if both defendants committed the same crime in response to the same acts of the same government agent. The objective test addresses this discrepancy by eliminating the evaluation of the individual defendant.

Answer A supports the subjective test. The subjective test specifically evaluates the individual defendant's culpability; the objective test explicitly disregards the individual defendant. The objective test may result in the acquittal of guilty people as a cost of preventing police excesses. A basic premise of the objective test is that even reasonable people can be induced to commit crimes in extreme situations. The objective test examines whether an average person would have committed the crime as a result of the government's actions. The subjective test, however, is premised upon the idea that only a person who was already predisposed to commit a crime would be induced to do so. **Answer C also supports the subjective test**, not the objective test. Law enforcement officials argue that many techniques are necessary to detect certain types of criminal activity. Crimes occurring between consenting, private parties are particularly difficult to discover. Use of undercover police officers and informants may be vital for law enforcement officials to be able to effectively catch criminals, particularly in the drug trade. Although law enforcement officers need a great deal of latitude to be able to effectively perform their jobs, the objective test attempts to create guidelines restricting their behavior. Therefore, **answer D is not the best answer.**

180.   **Answer D is the best answer.** Although prior criminal acts are not normally admissible against a defendant to prove a propensity to commit a crime, they may be used to counter a defense of entrapment under the majority, subjective test. When offered for that purpose, the evidence is not used to show a propensity; rather, the prior acts are given to show a defendant's predisposition, or willingness, to commit a crime. *United States v. Mayfield*, 771 F.3d 417 (7th Cir. 2014).

    Although **answer A may seem to be the best answer**, because it is the only choice that does not relate to Wayne's criminal record, it is not. As the government may introduce evidence of prior crimes in order to show a predisposition to commit a crime, the evidence in **answers B and C** would also be admissible. Wayne's drug possession conviction would be admissible, even though it is not the same crime as the one with which he is currently charged. The courts allow a wide range of evidence to be introduced to show that a person was predisposed to commit a crime. The possession conviction and the current charge of selling marijuana are both drug charges, and the possession conviction is recent. Thus, a court would likely allow the previous conviction to be admitted to show Wayne's predisposition to sell drugs. *Thomas v. Sec'y, Fla. Dep't. of Corr.*, 2020 WL 6060953 (M.D. Fla. 2020). Because the evidence listed in **answers A and C** would both be admissible, **answer B is not the best answer.** Even though Wayne's conviction for selling drugs was three years ago, the courts take a broad view of evidence that may be used to show a predisposition to commit a crime. Wayne's prior willingness to sell drugs may show that he was inclined to do so again. Once admitted into evidence, the jury must determine whether the defendant was led by the government action or whether he was already willing to commit the crime. **Answer C is not right** because the evidence in **answers A and B** would also be admissible.

181.   **Answer A is the best answer.** The defense of entrapment is not allowed in connection with a serious, violent crime. Mo. Rev. Stat. § 562.066(2). Thanh could not be charged with murder since the crime was not completed. Nonetheless, she could be properly convicted of attempted murder. Because Thanh is barred from using the defense of entrapment due to the nature of the violent crime committed, **answer B is not the correct answer.** Police encouragement of murder, particularly in allowing it to progress to the stage that it did with Thanh, exceeds the bounds of what society expects from law enforcement. However, under both tests, the courts assume law-abiding citizens will not attempt murder and thus cannot raise the entrapment defense. Thus, **answer C is not the best answer.** Regardless of whether the test looks to the defendant's predisposition, or focuses on the behavior of law enforcement officials, the entrapment defense cannot be successfully raised in connection with a charge of attempted murder as a matter of law. Whether or not Thanh would have committed the criminal act absent police encouragement is legally irrelevant. **Answer D is the wrong answer.**

182.   **Answer D is the best answer.** Courts consider a variety of factors in determining whether the entrapment defense is available to third parties. *State v. Nero*, 1 A.3d 184 (Conn.

App. Ct. 2010). In this case, Noah's continued participation in the drug lab was vital to the operation. Without Noah, there would have been no drugs and no need for Farah to assist with the distribution. Because Farah would not have become involved in Duane's business without Noah's inducement, she would likely be able to rely on the entrapment defense.

Answer A is not correct. Although Duane was not acting on behalf of the government, Noah was. Duane used the lab's successful operations to induce Farah to work there in connection with Noah. The success of the lab was the direct result of Noah's participation. It would be unreasonable to deny Farah the entrapment defense simply because she was directly approached by Duane instead of his "partner" Noah. Though Farah was willing to participate, that is not the important question. With the subjective test, courts ask whether the defendant was predisposed. Under the objective test, a determination must be made whether the government inducement was so extreme as to risk criminal actions by the reasonable citizen. Therefore, **answer B is not the best answer. Answer C is wrong.** Courts do not automatically extend the entrapment defense to all defendants—the defense is "defendant specific." Courts consider whether the particular individual was entrapped, looking either to her state of mind, or the inducement as to her.

183. No. Entrapment law, under the majority test, uses a subjective analysis that primarily considers the predisposition of the defendant to commit the crime charged. In this case, Louis had a reputation as a smuggler and boasted that he could smuggle anything into the country. The government can introduce evidence to show that Louis was willing and able to smuggle the antiques into the country. From that evidence, the jury could find, beyond a reasonable doubt, that Louis was predisposed to smuggle prior to the officer's request. On this basis, Louis could not raise a successful entrapment defense in most jurisdictions.

184. The objective (minority) test focuses on the behavior of the government. Even if Louis was predisposed to commit the crime, he could be acquitted using the entrapment defense if the government's behavior was sufficiently extreme as to likely cause crimes by a reasonable person. *People v. Akhmedov*, 825 N.W.2d 688 (Mich. Ct. App. 2012). In this case, the government official only placed an order on one occasion after one request. No money was even exchanged. The idea that the government was encouraging illegal smuggling may be disturbing. However, it may be difficult to prove that Louis was already a smuggler without hiring him to smuggle something into the country. Moreover, such actions would not induce a reasonable person to engage in illegal smuggling. Louis's entrapment claim will likely fail under the minority, objective test.

Entrapment is a defense based upon policy considerations. Therefore, the trier of fact must decide whether the government's behavior should be excused in order to facilitate the conviction of a person who engages in a troubling trade. Here, Louis is unlikely to successfully offer a defense of entrapment under either test.

INTOXICATION

185.   **The best answer is answer B.** Although *voluntary* intoxication cannot serve generally as an affirmative defense, in some states one may use evidence of such intoxication to negate one of the elements of the crime charged. *State v. Coker*, 412 N.W.2d 589 (Iowa 1987). As a matter of public policy, most jurisdictions have decided that it would be improper to allow a complete defense of voluntary intoxication because such a defense would permit a drunken person to legally commit acts that he would be held criminally responsible for if sober. Nonetheless, the criminal law is based on individual culpability for actions. It generally allows a defendant's intoxication to be considered to the extent that he had impaired judgment. On this ground, some jurisdictions allow evidence of intoxication to be admitted to demonstrate that a defendant did not possess the crime's requisite state of mind. A defendant may escape liability because the prosecution is unable to prove the necessary mental state for the crime, but not because intoxication provides a general defense to the criminal charge. Thus, **answer A is incorrect** in some jurisdictions. As explained above, the defendant would not be prohibited from introducing his intoxication to negate a state of mind requirement. However, in some states by statute, intoxication cannot be introduced as evidence for any reason in connection with any charge. The constitutional challenge to this rule was rejected by the Supreme Court in *Montana v. Egelhoff*, 518 U.S. 37 (1996). **Answer D is incorrect** because it looks to the government's failure to prove an element of the charge, rather than as an affirmative defense, which is what the question asked. **Answer C**, which suggests that a constitutional limit may be present in this case, **is wrong.** While the Supreme Court has held that laws that punish drug addicts (and possibly alcoholics) merely for their status as addicts violate the Constitution, these individuals can still be criminally sanctioned for the acts that they commit, as discussed earlier. *Robinson v. California*, 370 U.S. 660 (1962).

186.   Although evidence of intoxication could not be used as a general defense to the crime, Reese could escape liability in some states if his intoxication precluded the prosecution from establishing one or more of the requirements for the charged crime. Evidence of intoxication could allow the defense attorney to create a reasonable doubt that Reese had the requisite state of mind to commit the charged crime. Because reckless behavior can establish the state of mind requirement for various homicide offenses, the fact that Reese became inebriated would not likely defeat all homicide charges. The finder of fact could well conclude that Reese acted in a grossly reckless fashion by drinking so heavily, thereby causing the death. Given this possibility, and the availability of lesser charges such as involuntary manslaughter, it seems unlikely that Reese would escape criminal liability altogether.

187.   **Answer C is correct.** In some states, evidence of intoxication is allowed to negate the mental state element of the crime, particularly if it is a high state of mind, classified at common law, as specific intent. Inchoate offenses, such as attempted murder, are specific intent crimes. **Answer D is, therefore, wrong.**

Answer A is incorrect because it instructs the jury as if the defendant's intoxication, in and of itself, is a defense. **Answer B is not the best answer** because in no state is voluntary intoxication classified as a true defense. Rather, evidence of voluntary intoxication may be relevant to show that the defendant did not possess the necessary state of mind.

188. **Answer A is the best answer** because Brandi involuntarily consumed a strong drug that caused her to lose control and kill. Involuntary intoxication operates as a true defense. *Richards v. State*, 2015 WL 4503971 (Alaska App. 2015).

    Answer B is not the right answer because while Brandi chose to drink punch, she did not choose to consume an illicit drug, one which she could have known had a chance of leading to unusual behavior. **Contrary to answer C,** involuntary intoxication can present a defense in a prosecution for a person who takes a substance without knowledge or reason to know that it was intoxicating in nature. Involuntary intoxication could also be a defense if a person was forced to take an intoxicating substance against her will. **Answer D is incorrect** because Brandi may rely on the defense of involuntary intoxication if she drank voluntarily, but without knowledge of the substance in the punch.

189. **Yes,** for the defense of involuntary intoxication is based upon the view that if an individual is wholly without fault in consuming the affecting substance, she ought not to be held criminally responsible. If she has been forewarned, even if she did not fully believe the warning, it would have been utterly irresponsible of her to go ahead and drink a large amount of the suspect beverage. In such a situation, the intoxication would not likely be seen as involuntary and such a defense would fail.

THE INSANITY DEFENSE

190. **The best answer is answer B.** This response correctly identifies the so-called *M'Naughten* test, followed in a majority of jurisdictions. *Kassa v. State*, 485 P.3d 750 (Nev. 2021). The test, also known as the "right/wrong test," demands that the defendant, at the time of the crime, not know the difference between right and wrong because of his mental condition. One of the main criticisms of the *M'Naughten* test is that it does not accurately encompass different kinds of mental illnesses. The test focuses exclusively on mental illnesses resulting in cognitive failures. For example, the test does not consider a mentally ill person who understood that killing someone is wrong, even though she was unable to conform her behavior to that knowledge. Such criticism led to the adoption of a new test, the "irresistible impulse" test used in **answer C.** This test, used in a minority of jurisdictions, also has its critics, for it focuses exclusively on control and avoids issues concerning cognition or awareness.

    Answer A is incorrect in that it invokes the so-called "product test," also known as the *Durham* rule. *Durham v. United States*, 214 F.2d 862 (D.C. Cir. 1954) *abrogated by United States v. Brawner*, 471 F.2d 969 (D.C. Cir). This test requires that the jury determine whether the disease *caused* the crime, a determination even mental health professionals usually cannot make with certainty. Few states retain this test. **Answer D** sets out the Model Penal Code's approach to the insanity defense. This test allows for a person not to be held responsible for an action, even if he knows the action is wrong, if he does not have "substantial capacity" to "appreciate" the moral significance of the act. *State v. Carpio*, 43 A.3d 1 (R.I. 2012). This rule combines both the right/wrong analysis and the irresistible impulse rule. In these ways, the Model Penal Code approach is thought to give the jury the greatest role to determine the culpability of the defendant, which helps to reduce the problem of expert witnesses usurping the role of the jury in determining culpability.

191.   **Yes.** Under the right/wrong formulation of *M'Naughten*, the judge need only admit evidence that relates to the one specific question, namely whether the defendant knew that his actions were right or wrong. If, as stated above, Fernando understood the killing was wrong and knew that it was illegal, then the evidence of his justification could be excluded as irrelevant. *Commonwealth v. Bruno*, 407 A.2d 413 (Pa. Super. Ct. 1979).

192.   **The correct answer is answer A.** Expert testimony in insanity defense cases can be extremely helpful. Typically, however, experts are precluded from testifying to the ultimate question of insanity; that issue is for the trier of fact. Fed. R. Evid. 704(b). Testimony by an expert as to whether Fernando suffered from a mental disease and whether that disease caused the killing is outside the scope of proper examination of a witness. It would be unlikely that a judge would allow such testimony from an expert. Thus, **answer D is wrong.**

Answer B is incorrect, as the *M'Naughten* rule actually requires that the killing be undertaken because of the mental defect. As such, the determination as to whether Fernando's mental illness caused him to kill is of vital importance. An expert's testimony in this regard would be excluded, but not because it is irrelevant. **Answer C is also incorrect.** As noted above, while the jury must determine if the defendant meets the insanity standard, conclusory expert testimony is excluded because the jurors must make those determinations themselves.

193.   **Answer B is the best answer.** This was the holding of the United States Supreme Court in *Clark v. Arizona*, 548 U.S. 735 (2006) The Justices reasoned that "history shows no deference to *M'Naughten* that could elevate its formula to the level of fundamental principle, so as to limit the traditional recognition of a State's capacity to define crimes and defenses." **Answer C, of course, is then clearly incorrect. Answer A is also wrong** because the changed standard raised a constitutional issue, even though the government prevailed on the point. The legislature historically has been given the power to alter court rulings, so long as such rulings were not based upon constructions of the Constitution. As a consequence, **D is not correct.**

194.   **True.** Unlike other affirmative defenses such as self-defense, where some states put the burden on the defendant and others require the state to disprove the defense, the burden of proof as to insanity lies with the defendant in most jurisdictions. Typically, the state must prove the defendant's guilt beyond a reasonable doubt. At that point, the burden shifts to the defendant to demonstrate the requirements of the insanity defense, usually by a preponderance of the evidence. In the federal system, however, the defendant must prove the insanity defense by clear and convincing evidence, an even higher standard. 18 U.S.C. § 17. Legislatures have imposed particularly stringent requirements on those seeking to invoke the insanity defense for a variety of reasons, largely because of the widespread belief that the insanity defense may be too easily achieved. In fact, the insanity defense is seldom invoked and is rarely successful.

195. **Answer C is correct.** Most jurisdictions do not allow a judge to raise the insanity defense over the objections of the defense, even if a judge feels that such an action is appropriate. Unless the defendant is not competent to make the decision, the determination is to be made by him and his lawyer. *United States v. Marble*, 940 F.2d 1543 (D.C. Cir. 1991). **Answers A and B reflect the older approach to this problem.** Traditionally, the judge was either obligated, or at least permitted, to instruct on the defense if she saw evidence that might convince a reasonable person that the defendant met the requirements for the insanity defense. **Answer D is incorrect,** as the basis of the law here is not the probability of the success of the defense. Rather, the focus here is on which person has the right to make that decision.

DIMINISHED CAPACITY

196. **Answer C is the best answer.** Evidence of mental illness can be used to defeat the government's showing of state of mind, often referred to as diminished capacity. *State v. Horton*, 2020 WL 3267209 (Tenn. Crim. App. 2020). In contrast to the insanity defense, which asserts that the defendant committed the crime but should not be held responsible because of mental illness, a claim of diminished capacity states that the defendant could not be found guilty of the crime because she lacked the mental ability to form the requisite state of mind (e.g., intent or premeditation). Here, if the jury decides that Abigail was mentally incapable of premeditation, it cannot find her guilty of first degree murder. This would be true even if Abigail does not meet the jurisdiction's insanity requirements. Therefore, **answers B and D are incorrect.** Such evidence is relevant to the government's charge of murder. The first-degree murder charge would fail for lack of proof if the defendant did not have the required state of mind, regardless of whether or not the insanity defense was raised. **Answer A is wrong** because evidence from friends and family may be helpful in an effort by the defense lawyer to cast doubt on a defendant's state of mind. The defendant at trial is allowed to paint a full picture of her mental state, particularly if lay testimony is supplemented by expert testimony. *Commonwealth v. Larkins*, 489 A.2d 837 (Pa. Super. Ct. 1985).

197. **No special instruction on the evidence is required in this instance.** If the jury finds beyond a reasonable doubt that the government has shown all of the elements of the crime, including the mental state requirement, Abigail will be convicted. Because the insanity

defense is not being raised and is not available for the jury's consideration, special consideration need not be given to the evidence of her mental illness in this case. Just as a special instruction concerning misidentification or alibi would be unnecessary, no special instruction is necessary here. A judge may hesitate in delivering a special instruction on this evidence as it might give such evidence undue influence over evidence of equal merit (e.g., an alibi or physical evidence), tending to cast doubt upon the government's case. However, most judges are given the discretion as to whether to offer a jury instruction on this issue. If the judge feels that there is some confusion on this difficult issue, she may instruct the jury on the above information. *State v. Jackson*, 714 P.2d 1368 (Kan. 1986).

198. **Answer D is the best answer,** as the courts have consistently determined that evidence of mental illness can create confusion and misunderstanding on the part of the jurors. As a result, the state may constitutionally determine that evidence of mental illness may only be permitted when the defendant raises the defense of insanity, *Clark v. Arizona*, 548 U.S. 735 (2006). Several states have such restrictive rules. *Metrish v. Lancaster*, 569 U.S. 351 (2013). Thus, **answer A is not right. Answer B, then, is wrong** for the ruling in *Clark* was limited to evidence concerning mental disease. **Answer C is also wrong** because the discretion of trial judges is actually fairly limited by the rules of evidence, particularly as to evidence that would aid the defense.

COMPETENCY TO STAND TRIAL

199. **The best answer is answer D.** A defendant may be found incompetent to stand trial if she cannot understand the nature of the proceedings against her or if she cannot consult with her lawyer with a reasonable degree of rational understanding. *Dusky v. United States*, 362 U.S. 402 (1960). Competency and insanity are not exclusive of one another. That is, a person who was legally insane at the time of the crime may also be considered incompetent at the time of trial, but the evaluation of each issue remains distinct. With the evidence involved here—Sarah's deteriorating mental state—competency should be raised in order to gain consideration of this evidence before trial. **Answer C is incorrect** because the competency matter must be resolved before trial, before any other substantive legal questions can be answered, and because this evidence goes more to a competency issue than to an insanity defense. For this same reason, **answers A and B are incorrect.** This evidence should not be delayed until trial, to be used in evaluating Sarah's guilt or innocence. Although the evidence might be relevant as to several points if she is declared competent to stand trial, her competency must first be determined.

200. **True.** The issue of competency to stand trial arises when the defendant's *current* mental capacity is in question. This can be distinguished from the insanity defense and diminished capacity, both of which focus on the defendant's mental state at the time of the crime.

Practice Final Exam

201. **The best answer is B.** If the government is able to prove that Carolina intended to kill Fritz, she most likely would be convicted of voluntary manslaughter. This crime involves a killing "in the heat of passion," in which the individual intends to kill the victim, but only as a result of an extreme emotional exchange of some kind, such as a violent argument. The rule is that the exchange must be a legally adequate provocation. *Commonwealth v. Camacho*, 36 N.E.3d 533 (Mass. 2015). While words alone would not generally be enough to constitute a legally adequate provocation, words plus the slap might be sufficient. **Answer A is incorrect** because Carolina does not seem to have acted with premeditation.

If the government demonstrates that Carolina intended to kill Fritz, a conviction for negligent homicide is not the probable outcome. This charge requires only a negligence standard, not intent, and usually applies to accidental killings. Thus, **answer C is not the best answer. Answer D is not right** because voluntary intoxication provides no true defense under the law. Evidence of intoxication might be used to raise a doubt as to whether the defendant was able to form the requisite intention to commit a crime. On these facts, however, the government has likely proven intent, so Carolina's intoxication will be of no assistance to her case.

202. While Javier tried and tried to burn the neighbor's house down, he was not able to light a fire. A fire is an element of the crime of arson. It is not enough to come close — there must actually be some sort of fire [or in some states, an explosion] for there to be an arson conviction. Ohio Rev. Code § 2909.03.

203. Javier committed the crime of attempted arson. He wanted to burn the house down, and he took a very substantial step toward the completion of the crime of arson, thus attempting that offense.

204. The best answer is A. The only evidence that suggests that Ken intended the crime be committed is that he took Danny to the station and did not object. This evidence could just as easily lead to the conclusion that Ken only wanted to get away from the actual criminal as soon as possible. Ken was in a dangerous situation and probably feared for his life. Under such circumstances, there would be insufficient evidence of an agreement, which is the essence of the crime of conspiracy. *State v. Huntley*, 171 A.3d 1003 (R.I. 2017). Thus, **answer D is incorrect.**

Answer B refers to the defense of withdrawal, which is not available in all jurisdictions. Even if such a defense is accepted in his jurisdiction and if Ken otherwise is found to have been a conspirator, a claim that he had withdrawn from the conspiracy would fail. Jurisdictions that allow withdrawal as a defense would also require that Ken communicate his withdrawal to Danny or try to prevent the crime. His claim might have prevailed if Ken had reported the robbery to the police immediately after leaving the gas station. Therefore, **answer B is incorrect. Answer C is incorrect as well.** While it details Ken's involvement in the crime, the essential finding for a conspiracy conviction is that there was an agreement to carry out the crime. Such an agreement is not present here.

205. Yes. This history would make a finding of agreement much more likely. If Ken was aware that Danny was a criminal, it could make his decision to pick up Danny appear to be part of a plan. Any attempt by Ken to claim that he acted only under duress would seem less credible because Ken intentionally placed himself in a dangerous situation. In addition, the fact that the two knew each other and had a shared history of committing these sorts of crimes is more strongly suggestive of an agreement. The finding of an agreement would only be inferred from all of the circumstances. Nevertheless, if a jury finds an agreement from the actions of Ken and Danny, either explicit or implicit, Ken would be found guilty of conspiracy. *Direct Sales Co. v. United States*, 319 U.S. 703 (1943).

206. The best answer is A. Under the felony murder rule, as it exists in most states, liability will extend to any foreseeable death that results from the committed felony, and will allow for a conviction of felony murder. *People v. Davis*, 66 N.E.3d 1076 (N.Y. 2016). The reason for such a conviction is to hold criminals responsible for the consequences of their dangerous actions, even if there are unintended consequences. The rule applies to forcible felonies, like kidnapping, because these crimes are by nature so dangerous that a consequential loss of life is said to be generally foreseeable.

Answers B and C are incorrect. Whether Matt intended for Tamara to die is not the focus of the felony murder rule. The key inquiries under the felony murder rule are whether any inherently dangerous felony was intended and whether the death occurred during the commission of that felony. Here, Matt intended to commit kidnapping, he did so, and Tamara was killed while he carried out his felonious purpose. **Answer D is wrong** because the felony murder rule eliminates inquiry into intent. Moreover, accidents are foreseeable when transporting victims in kidnapping schemes.

207. The best answer is B. As a co-conspirator, Warrenetta can be held responsible for the foreseeable actions of her co-conspirator. *Pinkerton v. United States*, 328 U.S. 640 (1946). This policy of holding members of a conspiracy accountable for the actions of their partners will lead a trier of fact to find her guilty of murder. Even though the plan was not to use weapons, it is often held that weapons are foreseeable even with a contrary

understanding. **Answer A is incorrect** because Warrenetta is only responsible if the death was foreseeable.

Answer D is wrong. Warrenetta, as a co-conspirator engaged in a kidnapping, will face the same legal consequences as Matt. It is without significance that the killing with a gun by Matt was accidental because the broad rule as to criminal liability applies. Co-conspirators are held responsible for the foreseeable acts that take place. Therefore, **answer C is also incorrect.**

208. **No.** It is not enough that Kevin was angered by Dai's silly antics. In order to raise successfully a self-defense claim, Kevin would need to show both that he genuinely believed that force was necessary to protect himself and that this belief was reasonable. *Brown v. State*, 2017 WL 2304384 (Fla. Dist. Ct. App. 2017). Under the facts presented, neither can be shown.

209. **Answer C is the best answer.** Evidence of a defendant's mental illness can be used in furtherance of an insanity defense. It can also be used to demonstrate a failure of proof, in an attempt to negate the intent element of the crime, under the so-called diminished capacity doctrine. *Martin v. Pszczolkowski*, 2021 WL 3833728 (W. Va. 2021). Evidence of Alice's condition was therefore relevant to issues at trial. In effect, the defense strategy may have been to claim that because of her mental illness, she was unable to form the requisite intent to agree to a conspiracy or to rob the bank. Such an approach can be viewed as an assertion that the government has failed to prove all of the necessary elements, a failure of proof claim. Therefore, **answer A is incorrect.** Conspiracy requires proof that the defendant intended to agree to commit some crime, and as such, the ability of a defendant to form such intention is relevant. Thus, **answer B is wrong. Answer D is not right** because the evidence as presented does not necessarily compel such a finding. It is important to note that in a number of states, testimony as to mental illness can only be received in evidence if an insanity defense is offered. In such jurisdictions, the theory of diminished capacity is not permitted. *Metrish v. Lancaster*, 569 U.S. 351 (2013).

210. **The best answer is A.** Courts today hold that a judge does not have the ability to raise the insanity defense over the defendant's objection. *Phenis v. United States*, 909 A.2d 138 (D.C. 2006). A court must defer to a defendant's knowing decision to waive the insanity defense if a competent defendant made that decision intelligently and voluntarily. Therefore, **answer D is wrong.** Competency issues must be raised prior to trial. *Pate v. Robinson*, 383 U.S. 375 (1966). Because Alice's case was being presented to the jury for a verdict, Alice must have already been deemed competent to stand trial. Therefore, **answer B is incorrect. Answer C is also incorrect.** Here the defendant contended through the course of trial that she was not guilty and that the government could not prove its case against her. To then have the jury presented with an entirely contradictory instruction from the judge on the insanity defense, which generally presumes guilt as its premise, could certainly be seen as harmful to the defendant's cause.

211. The first question, which asked if the defendant suffered from a mental illness, might be considered acceptable. The second, however, would generally be considered impermissible. Concerns about expert testimony are especially pervasive in the context of the insanity defense. The difficulty is that the *jury* must find whether or not the defendant qualifies as insane. Especially in instances of complex technical or professional evidence, juries are thought to be prone to give too much weight to the testimony of an expert and, in effect, allow the expert opinion to determine the outcome of the case. For this reason, courts and lawmakers have attempted to exclude from expert testimony anything that speaks to the "ultimate issue." *United States v. Shaffer*, 472 F.3d 1219 (10th Cir. 2007). The second question is precisely the question that the jury needed to answer, and the expert should not have been permitted to answer it. The first question, though, is more complicated as it goes directly to the witness's expertise based on his professional evaluation of the defendant. Many courts would allow the expert to answer this question.

212. Shopkeepers do not generally owe any duty of warning to customers in connection with the sale of lawful products. Still, under the homicide offenses of murder (implied malice) or manslaughter (involuntary) all persons are prohibited from engaging in reckless behavior that causes death. Walt may not have understood, at the start, what was happening with the large number of teens buying household cleaning products. Nonetheless, he certainly was made aware of the phenomenon when he spoke with his son. As a result, he could be found to have been consciously aware of the great risk created by the continued sale of these products. By not only selling the items, but also increasing his stock in them, he could be found criminally responsible for involuntary manslaughter, or perhaps even for second degree murder. *Coyle v. Commonwealth*, 653 S.E.2d 291 (Va. Ct. App. 2007).

213. **The best answer is answer A.** Betty was in a unique position to help Martin, being employed by him. As such, she was under a duty to come immediately to his assistance. Thus, she could be found guilty of manslaughter or even murder. *Commonwealth v. Pestinikas*, 617 A.2d 1339 (Pa. 1992). While a charge of negligent homicide would be one possible outcome of Betty's case, the facts could allow for a determination that Betty was more than merely negligent. Therefore, **answer B is not the best answer. Answer C is correct, but only in the abstract.** Although a duty to come to someone's assistance is generally not imposed in the criminal laws of this country, there are exceptions when the person is in a unique position to prevent harm to another. As Martin's nurse, Betty held such a position and could be found to be contractually and criminally responsible for his welfare. Her callous disregard for her patient's condition might indeed lead to a charge and conviction for a serious homicide offense. **Answer D** suggests that Betty did not cause Martin's death. The trier of fact could decide that withholding his medication and failing to provide prompt medical assistance did in fact cause his death.

214. Dirk and Eric would certainly raise a First Amendment challenge to prevent their convictions. Because their speech is politically motivated, they could not be convicted based upon the content of their message. *Kennedy v. City of Villa Hills*, 635 F.3d 210

(6th Cir. 2011). The First Amendment's protections would forbid such a prosecution on that basis. Localities can, however, place limitations on the location and volume of the speech. Thus, the First Amendment challenge will likely fail, with the state relying on the manner of the speech, not its content. The statute under which the state proposes to prosecute the two may have Fifth and Fourteenth Amendment Due Process problems. The so-called "void for vagueness" doctrine dictates that laws must be sufficiently clear to put the public on notice. A reasonable person must be able to discern the meaning of the code language. As it stands, it appears that this provision could be determined unconstitutional under the Due Process Clause. The scope of the law seems indeterminate, in particular, the definition of "loud, disturbing and unnecessary noise." *Tanner v. City of Virginia Beach*, 674 S.E.2d 848 (Va. 2009). Even if the law is upheld under Due Process scrutiny, the defendants could argue that, as applied, the statute is invalid as their speech was not "loud, disturbing and unnecessary" under the circumstances. The use of the powerful bull horns may discredit that argument. It may also demonstrate that the defendants intended to cause "public inconvenience, annoyance or alarm," as required, and not simply to offer an anti-government message.

215. **The correct answer is answer B.** At common law, the fleeing felon doctrine allowed an officer to shoot a suspect in order to prevent flight from the scene of a felony if the officer had probable cause to believe the suspect had committed a felony. The Supreme Court, however, has imposed a far stricter standard on law enforcement. *Tennessee v. Garner*, 471 U.S. 1 (1985). In order to raise a successful defense based on the need to stop the man from fleeing, the officer must show that the suspect posed a continuing serious danger to others. The commission of a burglary, as in *Garner*, is not enough to demonstrate such danger as burglars are often unarmed and do not threaten others. Here it appears that the suspect would not have posed any obvious danger to others simply because he was running and was likely a burglar. As such, **answers A and C are not the best answers. Answer D is also not right.** While an officer may only intend to wound a suspect to prevent further flight, criminal liability may be imposed if the officer kills the suspect or seriously injures him. In considering whether deadly force was necessary under the circumstances, the court will balance the competing interests at stake and determine that the government's interests in arresting an escaping burglar are outweighed by the individual suspect's interest in life and good health.

216. **The best answer is C.** If a child is alive even for a matter of moments, it is deemed to be a viable human being. Under the traditional definition of homicide — the killing of a human being by a human being — the actions of Adam would constitute murder. *State v. Lamy*, 969 A.2d 451 (N.H. 2009). **Answer A, therefore, is incorrect,** as no such showing of future life is required. **Answer B is wrong** for two reasons. First, as the father of the child, Adam clearly owed a duty of care to the infant. Second, it was not his failure to take care of the child that is the basis of the homicide prosecution. Rather, it was his affirmative action in suffocating the child that is the subject of the case. **Answer D is also wrong** because the standard rule is that to be a human being for homicide purposes the child must survive the birth process, even if only for a short period. Some states have enacted infanticide statutes, or laws that expand the definition of "human being" for homicide purposes. Ala. Code § 13A-6-1.

217. **The best answer is C.** The Supreme Court held that the entrapment defense is supposed to raise the issue of the defendant's state of mind at the moment when she is first contacted by a government agent, not later when the defendant seeks to act. *United States v. Jacobson*, 503 U.S. 540 (1992). Thus, **answer B is not right. Answer D** does not properly lay out the rule as to defenses and the burden of proof. It is up to the individual jurisdiction to determine upon whom the burden shall fall; there is no constitutional requirement that defenses must be disproved by the government, though some states do mandate that. **Answer A** correctly notes that the burden may be on the defendant, but it fails to look at the timing issue mentioned above.

218. **The best answer is D.** A conviction for rape requires the government to prove that the defendant, through force or threat of force, had intercourse with the victim without that person's consent. **Answer A is therefore wrong.** However, rape shield laws generally prohibit evidence of prior sexual encounters from being introduced by the defense. *See, e.g.*, Tenn. Rule of Evid. 412. One reason for such laws is to prevent the victim's character and sexual history from becoming the focus of the trial. In addition, even if the defendant demonstrates that the victim has had sex consensually with other partners, it would not necessarily follow that she consented to sex on the occasion in question. Hence, **answer B is not right. Answer C may otherwise be correct**, but as a result of rape shield laws, the defendant will be barred from even offering the evidence, so that **the better answer is answer D.**

219. **The best answer is C.** In most jurisdictions, an attempt offense can only be successful if the prosecution shows that the defendant took a substantial step toward the commission of the crime, or a step in close proximity to the crime. *United States v. Walker*, 990 F.3d 316 (3d Cir. 2021). Juana's steps were very early in the process; she could well have changed her mind before dousing the store with lighter fluid. Her actions were simply preparation, far short of what would be needed, even if her purpose was certain. **Answer A, then, is incorrect, as is answer B.** It is not the number of steps that determines if an attempt has been taken, but rather how substantial they are, or how close those steps get toward the commission of an offense. **Answer D, however, is wrong.** The law for the attempt offense does not require the execution of the last possible step prior to the completion of the crime. Such a rule would create too many dangers and prevent criminal actors from being halted.

220. **Yes.** With her purchase of the fluid, plus her presence at closing with a large bag, Juana may now be seen as having taken a substantial step or gotten dangerously close to the commission of the crime.

Index